Applying Successful Training Techniques

A Practical Guide To
Coaching And Facilitating Skills

Joe B. Wilson

San Francisco

ISBN: 0-7879-5092-0

Published by

350 Sansome Street, 5th Floor
San Francisco, California 94104-1342
(415) 433-1740; Fax (415) 433-0499
(800) 274-4434; Fax (800) 569-0443

Visit our website at: www.pfeiffer.com

Printing 10 9 8 7 6 5 4 3 2 1

ACKNOWLEDGMENTS

About The Author

Joe Wilson, a Vice President of Richard Chang Associates, Inc., is a training consultant and instructional media producer with more than 20 years of international experience. He has a broad background in the development of video, print, and computer-based instructional programs—from needs analysis through design, production, implementation, and evaluation. His experience in project management, development, and delivery of training programs spans a wide range—from highly technical systems projects, to management/sales development, to Total Quality implementations.

The author would like to acknowledge the support of the entire team of professionals at Richard Chang Associates, Inc. for their contribution to the guidebook development process. In addition, special thanks are extended to the many client organizations who have helped us shape the practical ideas and proven methods shared in this guidebook.

Additional Credits

Editor: Sarah Ortlieb Fraser and Ruth Stingley

Reviewers: P. Keith Kelly and Pamela Wade

Graphic Layout: Christina Slater and Dottie Snyder

Cover Design: John Odam Design Associates

Preface

The 1990's have already presented individuals and organizations with some very difficult challenges to face and overcome. So who will have the advantage as we move toward the year 2000 and beyond?

The advantage will belong to those with a commitment to continuous learning. Whether on an individual basis or as an entire organization, one key ingredient to building a continuous learning environment is *The Practical Guidebook Collection* brought to you by the Publications Division of Richard Chang Associates, Inc.

After understanding the future *"learning needs"* expressed by our clients and other potential customers, we are pleased to publish *The Practical Guidebook Collection.* These guidebooks are designed to provide you with proven, *"real-world"* tips, tools, and techniques—on a wide range of subjects—that you can apply in the workplace and/or on a personal level immediately.

Once you've had a chance to benefit from *The Practical Guidebook Collection,* please share your feedback with us. We've included a brief *Evaluation and Feedback Form* at the end of the guidebook that you can fax to us at (714) 727-7007.

With your feedback, we can continuously improve the resources we are providing through the Publications Division of Richard Chang Associates, Inc.

Wishing you successful reading,

Richard Y. Chang
President and CEO
Richard Chang Associates, Inc.

TABLE OF CONTENTS

"If you want one year's prosperity, grow grain, but if you want ten year's prosperity, grow men and women."

Anonymous

CHAPTER ONE

INTRODUCTION

You may not be a professional trainer. Yet, at some point in your life, you've been called upon to facilitate learning. It may go as far back as a younger sibling asking you to teach shoe tying. Or perhaps just last year your neighbor admired your landscaping and prodded you for gardening instructions. Maybe last week upper management assigned you to train a department in advanced computer skills.

On the other hand, you could very well be a professional trainer. Maybe you've sat through several classes on how to train, but it was years ago, even before the advent of videotape recorders. Or it wasn't *that* long ago, but the classes were heavy on theory, and light on practical application.

Odds are that you've had past training opportunities *(whether or not your background is in training)* and will be tasked with plenty more. Currently, many organizations are counting on individuals from all areas of operations to coach other employees. How well you handle these training opportunities will make a difference in both your organization and your career.

Why Read This Guidebook?

This guidebook reduces the complexity of training theory by providing a simple, successful method that any non-trainer, novice trainer, or seasoned trainer can use to develop successful training techniques. There's no heavy instructional prose, no complicated procedures, no technical lingo to wade through. If you're after effective ideas, solid examples, and successful results, read on.

Employees who are called upon or who take it upon themselves to teach or train within their organizations aren't trainers *per se*, rather they're coaches and facilitators. Their goal: coaching people to improve their job performance by facilitating learning.

If you've been put in that position, it's probably for a good reason. You may know the parameters of a particular job or content area better than your organization's training department or an outside trainer. Or, you may have especially strong communication skills and a proven track record of coaching successes. In either circumstance, if you can learn some of a professional trainer's techniques, you're right on course. That's where *Applying Successful Training Techniques* enters the picture.

Most experienced training professionals would agree that there is always room for improving presentation form and style. And, inevitably, your presentation skills and techniques will influence how those you're coaching evaluate your training and apply that training on the job, regardless of how well you've prepared the materials.

While this guidebook won't transform you into a full-fledged trainer, it will eliminate some of the common frustrations and anxieties that plague individuals tasked with facilitating learning. *Applying Successful Training Techniques* touches on planning, discusses delivery skills, encourages effective use of learning materials, and provides tips for presentation. And, it will help you develop presentation *flair.* It's your means to becoming an effective coach and facilitator.

Who Should Read This Guidebook?

This guidebook is not targeted at successful professional trainers, but if you fall into this group, odds are you'll pick up some useful tips by reading it. *Applying Successful Training Techniques* is aimed at individuals who have not had formal education in training but are still tasked with coaching and facilitating. They could be supervisors, managers, project managers, content experts, novice trainers, and so forth.

This guidebook may alter your thinking about how to coach people and facilitate learning. It should bolster your confidence by giving you essential techniques used by successful coaches and facilitators.

When And How To Use It

This guidebook can be your ticket to successful training. It depends upon how willing and dedicated you are to learning and practicing these techniques.

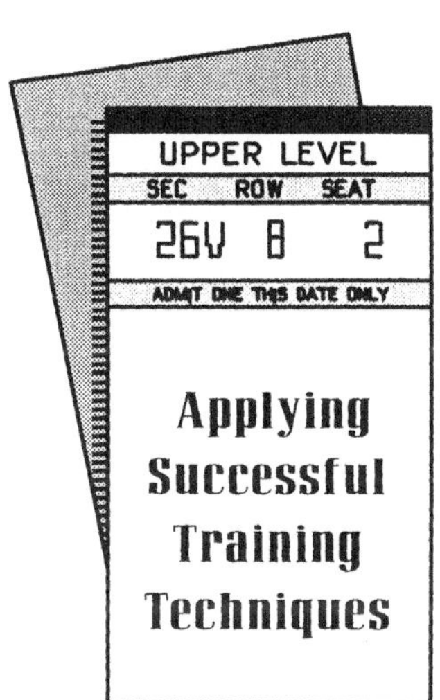

Perhaps no one in your organization has asked you about training your department, but you're interested in improving your employees' skills. Read through this guidebook. If you've been asked to train a new employee and doubt how well you can perform the task, check out the included tips. They'll ease the process.

If your organization's CEO has picked you as the content expert tasked with training fifteen corporate officers next week, study this guidebook immediately. Keep in mind that the training process starts before actual instruction occurs.

And while you may be able to skip some pages, such as those that apply to training groups when you're coaching one-on-one, at some point in your career you'll probably want to cover all the material. The minutes you spend studying how to improve your coaching and facilitating skills will result in hours and dollars saved down the line.

When And How To Use It

Developing Coaching And Facilitating Skills

No matter what your position in an organization, you'll have to assume training responsibilities at one time or another. Even if you have a corporate training department at your disposal, some training will fall within your job description. For example, have you ever been asked to train a new employee? Have you ever had to present a new program to your department? If so, you've been asked to facilitate learning.

Training is essential for helping employees contribute productively. As employees master new attitudes, skills, and knowledge, organizations ride the wave of a more productive work force.

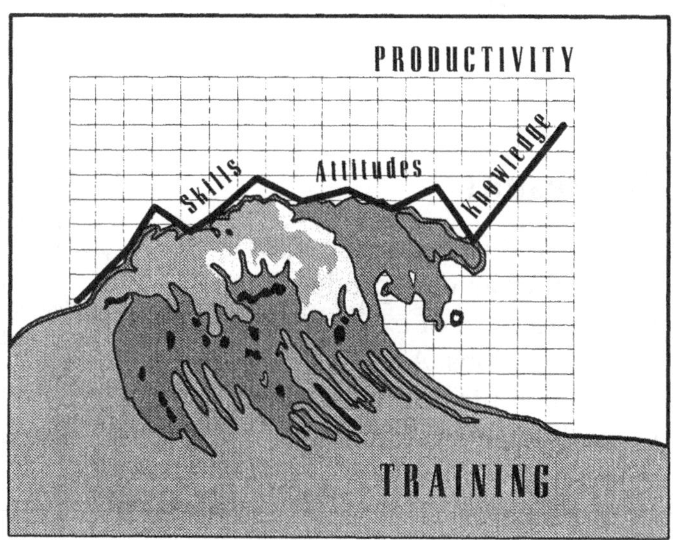

But not all training hits the mark. Training is more than mere *show and tell.* Expert trainers have mastered certain techniques. Their coaching and facilitating skills allow them to teach what needs to be learned in such a way that employees pick it up easily and use it successfully.

Who Needs Training?

Anyone who works will need training at one time or another. Why? Because organizations and technology change and evolve, demanding an increase or change in attitude, skills, and knowledge. As job descriptions, work processes, tools, and people change, you'll need to teach new skills, adjust attitudes, and help others acquire new knowledge.

What's The Result?

Effective coaching and facilitating boosts employees to a higher level of productivity. It allows employees to meet or exceed the quality standards set for their jobs. And, as employees see their contributions to the organization escalate, their morale increases. Some even set higher standards for themselves.

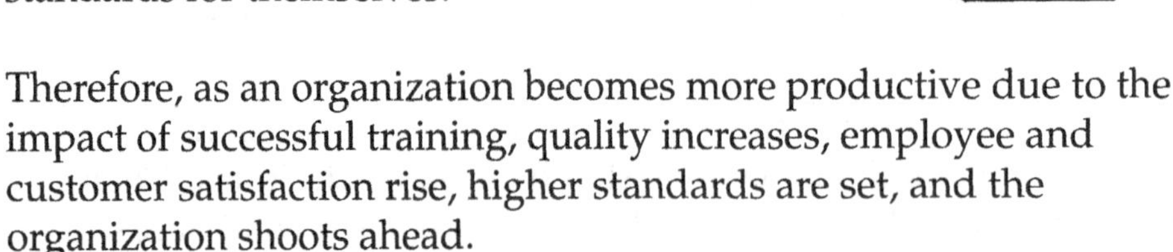

Therefore, as an organization becomes more productive due to the impact of successful training, quality increases, employee and customer satisfaction rise, higher standards are set, and the organization shoots ahead.

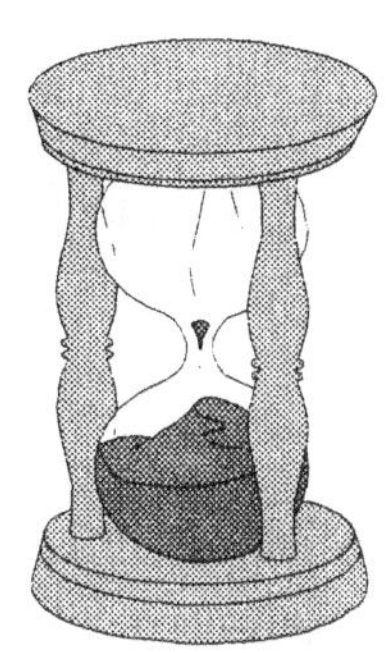

But it doesn't happen all at once. Taking an organization from mediocre to successful by employing effective training techniques takes time. Coaching and facilitating skills improve only through practice. But the small gains of steady, measurable progress can eventually snowball into organizational reform—thus making coaching and facilitating an exciting prospect.

How Do The Skills Help?

Don't put off mastering effective coaching and facilitating skills. Inevitably, you'll be called upon to train. And you want your efforts to prove successful. Many non-trainers believe that they can competently train an individual or group by simply sharing or showing how they've been able to master new knowledge, skills, or attitudes. It's not that simple.

To become an effective coach and facilitator, you first need to understand the adult learning process, then plan for success. You'll have to identify your trainees' attitudes, skills, and knowledge to know what you'll need to cover to get them up to speed. You'll need to map your approach and produce your materials. And, finally, how you apply your training techniques ultimately determines your success as a coach and facilitator. This success is calculated and tracked during and after the training.

Note: These are the phases in the High-IMPACT Training Model, which is covered in more detail in Chapter Four.

Chapter Two Worksheet: The Importance Of Coaching And Facilitating Skills

1. List any training you've done *(one-on-one or with a group)* in your current and/or previous organization *(e.g., computer training, operating a printing press, management skills, etc.)*.

2. Describe one of those training experiences *(e.g., who did it include, what was the purpose, how did it go, was it successful?)*.

3. Identify an employee or group in your organization who could use training, and explain the key areas that need improvement *(e.g., not a good team player, needs organizational skills, lower productivity than other work groups, too many errors, etc.).*

4. What benefits would be gained if the employee or group in Question # 3 were trained effectively?

How Do Adults Learn?

"You can't teach an old dog new tricks" is an adage that's been overused as an excuse for years. Actually, adults are exceptionally adept and flexible learners, if you follow some principles established through research by psychologists and other learning experts. Take the following principles into consideration and you'll multiply your success rate.

Principles Of Adult Learning

Anyone responsible for training others should be aware that adult learners have distinctive characteristics and needs. Once you understand the principles followed by those who teach adults, you'll find that facilitating learning is much easier than you anticipated. The following seven principles will give you a good grasp of how to handle adult learning:

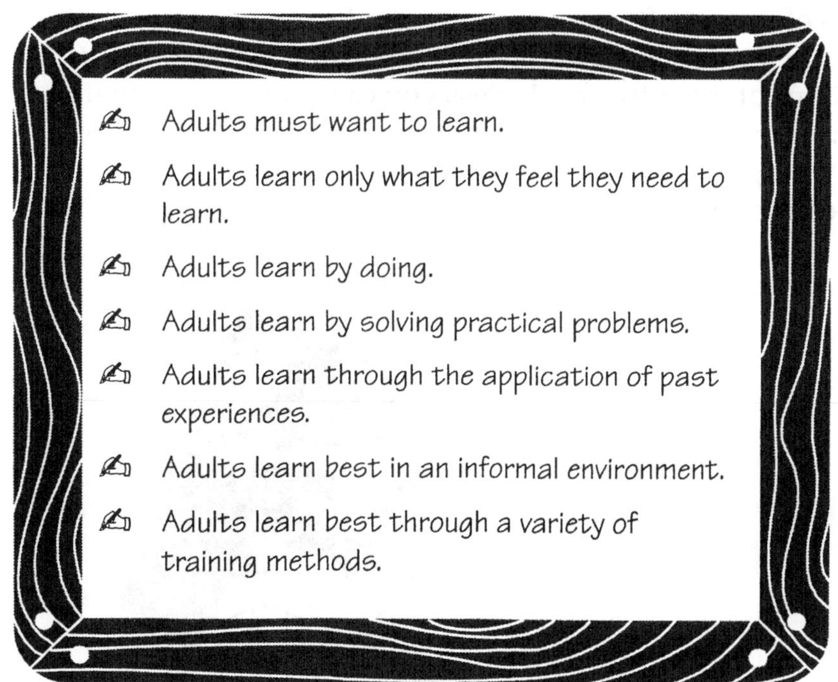

- Adults must want to learn.
- Adults learn only what they feel they need to learn.
- Adults learn by doing.
- Adults learn by solving practical problems.
- Adults learn through the application of past experiences.
- Adults learn best in an informal environment.
- Adults learn best through a variety of training methods.

Let's look at each of these principles and see how they can apply to coaching employees and facilitating learning in your organization.

Adults must want to learn

You can't shove learning down adults' throats. You *can* stand on your head to get their attention, but unless adults want to learn, they'll tune you out. If you're facing an individual who is resisting what you're trying to teach, provide evidence of why it's important to learn the material. Will it make the job easier? Will it improve skills and possibly result in a higher-paying job?

However, if you can't persuade someone to learn, you might be better off leaving that person alone. Otherwise, you'll waste your time and set yourself up for disappointment.

Adults learn only what they feel they need to learn

This principle emphasizes the importance of *sticking to the point.* If Mara, an accounting assistant, feels she only needs to learn the basics of a new software program, then focus on the key skills she needs to use on the job and briefly touch on the *"nice to have"* functions of the software. Unless you can convince her that learning the more advanced functions will make it easier for her to run her reports or enable her to advance in her career, stick to the immediate needs at hand.

Adults learn by doing

Adult learners aren't particularly disposed toward textbooks full of boring instruction. Hours of lecture also turn them off. Provide learners opportunities to actively participate in the learning process. Ensure that they apply their new skills or knowledge while you're coaching them.

Adults learn by solving practical problems

Don't inundate adult learners with hypothetical case examples that only support theories. Hit them with *real-world* problems and challenges. If you teach about their world, learning takes place naturally and effectively.

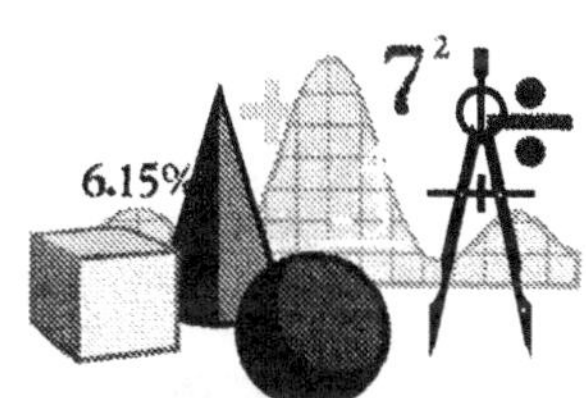

Adults learn through the application of past experiences

New knowledge must be related to, and integrated with, old knowledge. Point out any areas of similarity and provide a rationale for the change. This can prove challenging, however. If, for example, you're coaching an individual to learn a completely different way to inventory stock items, you may face resistance. Or the employee may listen, but revert to his old way of inventorying when he returns to the job. The key lies in helping the learner see the logical culminations of past experiences leading to new—and most likely improved—ways of doing things.

In addition, if you encourage your trainees to (1) provide feedback and (2) challenge content during training, you'll assist them in integrating the new information with past experiences.

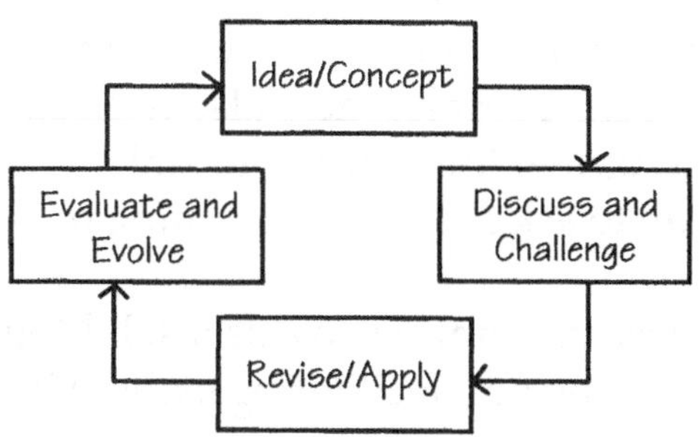

Adults learn best in an informal environment

Some adults have unpleasant memories of school days; you'd do best to avoid any type of grading, assigned seats, and strict rules. Seat your group in such a way that all involved can actively participate, and provide a means whereby all learners can measure their own progress during the training process. If you have a checklist of items they need to know, have them check off each item when it's mastered. Using humor and informal discussion are other techniques that help break the formal educational stigma of the *"traditional"* classroom.

Adults learn best through a variety of training methods

When feasible, use a variety of training methods in your approach. Statistics show that a combination of learning methods results in a higher level of learning than any single approach. For example, not all adults are auditory learners; many learn best by listening to and watching a video, then seeing someone demonstrate a task in person. Most learners also need hands-on participation or active discussion for learning to sink in. If you're coaching individuals, be sure to ask about their learning preferences.

These principles provide a solid foundation on which to build your coaching and facilitating skills. Once you understand that you can teach adult learners more effectively if you keep these principles in mind, you're ready to learn how training applies to three distinct areas of learning.

Types Of Learning

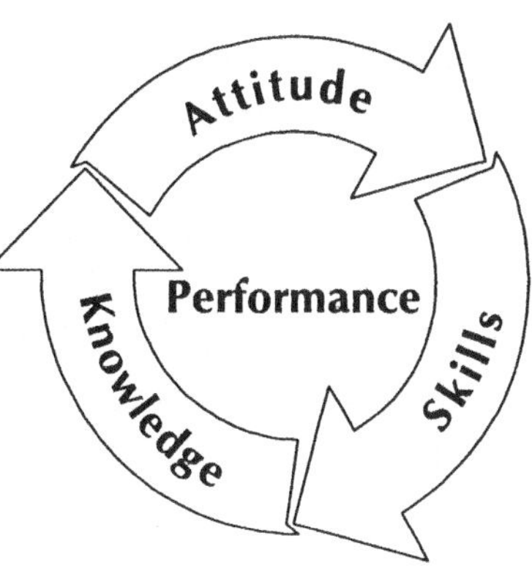

Many people aren't aware that training covers three distinct areas: attitude, skills, and knowledge. As an effective coach and facilitator, you will implement one, two, or all three of the areas, depending upon what behavioral or performance improvements your trainees need to achieve.

Attitude

In some cases, a change of attitude is necessary to improve productivity. Are customer service representatives rude to customers? Is a clerical worker not lending sufficient support because of an attitude problem? While both of these cases could possibly use knowledge or skills training, the problems won't go away until attitudes improve. Your coaching and facilitating skills are critical in these types of situations.

Skills

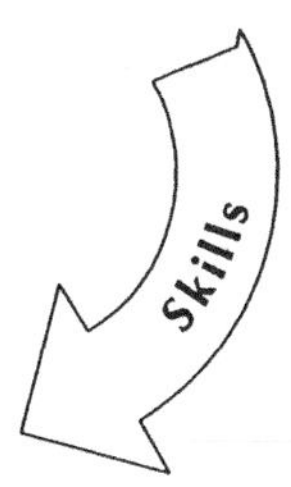

Skills-based training or coaching comes into play when new employees come on board, or changes in job descriptions or technology require the learning of new skills. It can also apply in situations where an employee hasn't quite mastered a skill. The key here is to clearly explain expected performance in measurable terms. For example, to tell Sylvia, a new garment worker in a clothing factory, that she must *"improve"* is not enough. She needs to know how many blouses to complete in an hour's time, and exactly what types of variations in fabric and workmanship are *"unacceptable."*

Skills training usually involves demonstration, practice, and feedback—either from you, another expert, or by some of the more sophisticated self-instructional multimedia programs.

You can also help individuals master a new skill by being available after the initial session(s) to coach them toward success. In a group setting, you can facilitate learning by allowing time for trial and error during the training. Once you set clear standards and expectations, skills training success is relatively easy to measure.

Knowledge

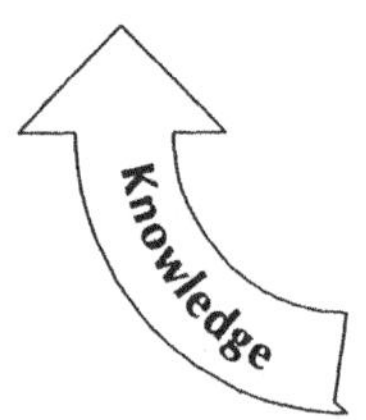

Knowledge instruction is often the foundation for performance improvement, yet adult learners sometimes resist this type of training. It can be seen as being dull, which frequently results in a low retention rate. Nevertheless, certain types of knowledge— such as concepts, facts, procedures, and policies —are critical to successful job completion. If you are attempting to facilitate knowledge learning, you must target it to your trainees' level, and be able to help them apply it to their jobs. Keep in mind that adult learners are pros at weeding out what is *"unnecessary"* information.

Coaching and facilitating are tools you can use to improve your employees' job performance. However, these tools will only be effective if they fit the needs of the adult learner and the categories of learning that translate into success on the job. The next chapter provides an overview of a practical process that enables you to use these tools competently.

Chapter Three Worksheet: Training Adults Effectively

1. Think back to a training situation in which you were the trainee. Rate your trainer on how well he or she followed the seven principles of adult learning. Give each item below a rating from 1 to 5. A score of 5 means the trainer followed that principle well, a 3 is average, and a 1 means the trainer didn't follow it at all.

☐ Taught what I wanted to learn

☐ Taught what I felt I needed to learn

☐ Helped me actively participate in the session

☐ Provided practical problems to solve

☐ Related new knowledge to my past experiences

☐ Provided an informal environment

☐ Used a variety of training methods

2. Choose two of the principles that received the lowest scores. What would you have done differently in the training session to make it more effective for adult learners?

3. Using the same situation you rated in Question # 1, consider whether the training improved your attitude, skills, and/or knowledge. How successful was the training in these three areas?

Attitude:

Skills:

Knowledge:

BECOMING A COACH AND FACILITATOR

Typically, training is much more complicated than simply demonstrating for someone how to perform a task, or getting up in front of a group and lecturing about some topic. In terms of purpose, your training should attempt to:

> *"Transfer specific attitudes, skills, and knowledge to those you are coaching or training in such a way that they can improve their job performance."*

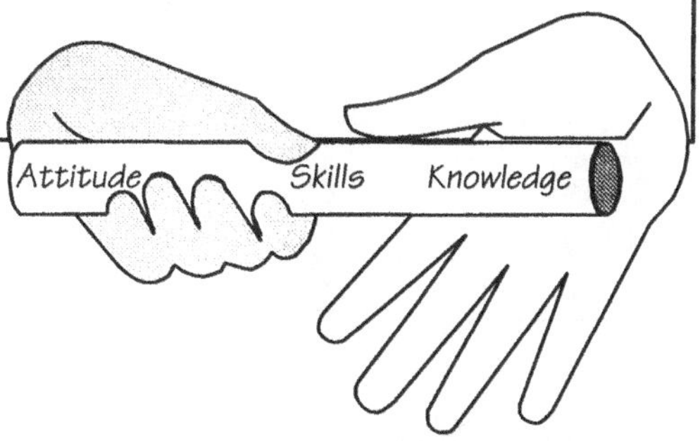

Your purpose isn't just to finish training an individual as quickly as possible so you can get back to your *"real"* job. Nor does it involve distributing a stack of handouts, hoping that the trainees you were asked to train will absorb the correct information. It doesn't even include a comprehensive effort to quiz a colleague on what you consider essential knowledge, *if* that knowledge will not actually help him improve his job performance.

Suddenly the scope of training takes on a new dimension. Unless those you are coaching truly improve their performance on the job, you've failed. Your success rate rests mainly on how well you're equipping employees or fellow workers to meet the demands of the organization and its customers.

But what does it take? Just how can you train others to improve their job performance?

Effective coaches and facilitators don't wing it. They have a plan—a blueprint that enables them to reach their goals for training. The following High-IMPACT Training™ Model is one such process you can use to make your training a success.

HIGH-IMPACT TRAINING™ MODEL

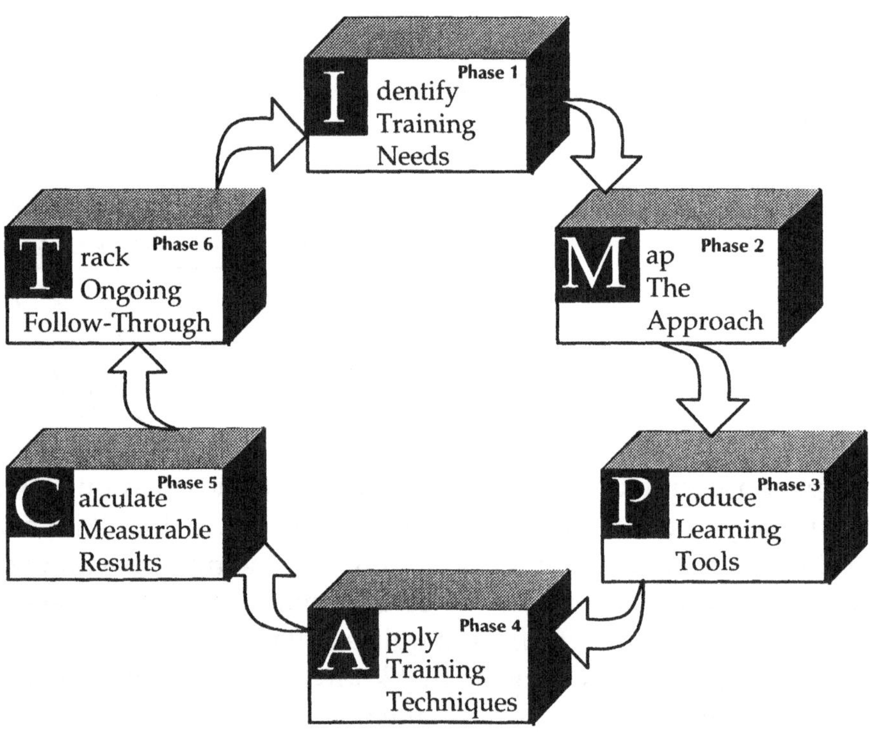

The High-IMPACT Training Model focuses on the importance of effective, targeted training. The following table illustrates what occurs during each of its six phases.

PHASE	DESCRIPTION
1. **I dentify Targeted Training Needs**	Determine if and how training can play a role in improving job performance; target training outcomes.
2. **M ap The Approach**	Choose the appropriate training approach(es) that will best support the targeted outcomes and improve job performance.
3. **P roduce Learning Tools**	Produce all training/coaching components (*e.g., materials, audiovisual aids, job aids,* etc.).
4. **A pply Training Techniques**	Deliver the training as designed to ensure successful results.
5. **C alculate Measurable Results**	Assess whether your training/coaching accomplished actual performance improvement; communicate the results, and redesign the process as necessary.
6. **T rack Ongoing Follow-Through**	Hone in on the techniques that individuals and organizations can use to ensure that the impact of their training does not diminish.

The High-IMPACT Training Model is a practical, effective approach to training. While this guidebook touches on the different phases, it specifically emphasizes Phase Four, which focuses on applying training techniques to increase your effectiveness in *delivering* training. You can plan carefully and extensively, but if your presentation is ineffective, your efforts will fall far short of success. So take care to practice the delivery and facilitation skills set forth in this guidebook.

Note: Each guidebook in the *High-IMPACT Training Series* focuses on various phases in the High-IMPACT Training Model. See the other guidebooks for tips on Phases One, Two, Three, Five, and Six.

You're on your way. You've taken the first step toward improving your coaching and facilitating skills by picking up this guidebook. You're now aware of the techniques that motivate adult learners, and you've taken a brief look at a six-phase approach to successful training. Keep going. More skills await!

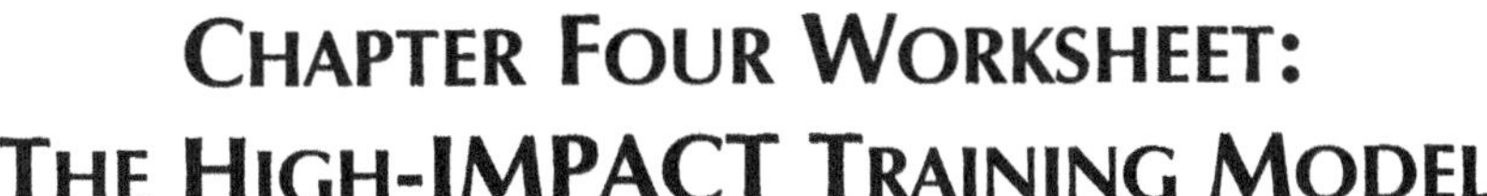

Chapter Four Worksheet: The High-IMPACT Training Model

1. Think back to a training session in which you were asked to train an individual or a group. Which of the six phases in the High-IMPACT Training Model do you feel you did well? Which phases could have used improvement?

2. Why is it so important to follow a structured process for coaching and facilitating?

CHAPTER FIVE

A Case Example: Nalu Surf

Nalu Surf, an ocean sports manufacturer/ retailer with headquarters in Honolulu, was founded by world-renowned surfboard shaper, Richard Ayer, in 1987. The company has grown from a home garage surfboard manufacturing entity to an international, $55 million-per-year company. Nalu Surf's vision is to be a *"leading worldwide manufacturer and retailer of high quality ocean sports equipment and clothing."* The company is presently ranked number four in the industry worldwide. It also faces some varied training challenges.

Nalu Surf manufactures surfboards and sailboards, then sells them in its retail outlets—along with wet suits, surfing accessories, sportswear, swimwear, and snorkeling gear purchased from third-party vendors for resale. The company has a total of 266 employees, and is managed as a fairly flat organization, with relatively few levels of employees.

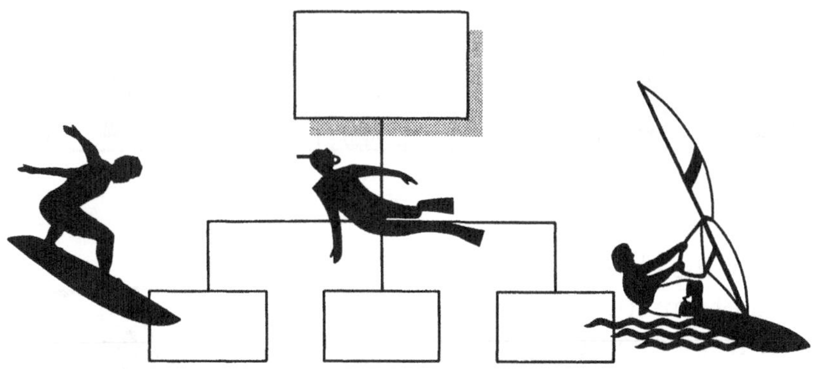

Customer service is a high priority in the organization. While customers are very satisfied with products and services, this comes at a price (*many free repairs, no-questions-asked returns, time-consuming consultations with customers for custom board manufacturing, etc.).* The sales force often feels as if it spends more time rectifying problems than selling new products.

Nalu Surf faces another difficult situation. It was recently fined by the city of Honolulu for violating toxic waste regulations *(ingredients for surfboard manufacturing, such as polystyrenes, require special handling)*. The ocean sports community is extremely sensitive about the environment, and this is a potential public relations nightmare.

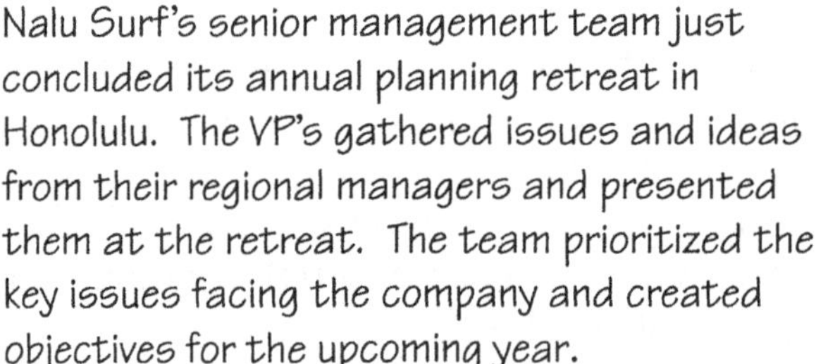
Nalu Surf's senior management team just concluded its annual planning retreat in Honolulu. The VP's gathered issues and ideas from their regional managers and presented them at the retreat. The team prioritized the key issues facing the company and created objectives for the upcoming year.

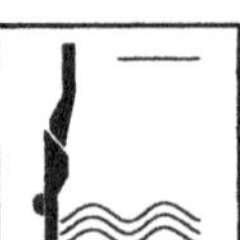

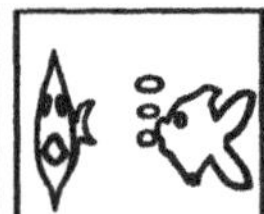

Several of the objectives dealt with the training of employees. And while an outside trainer could help in some instances, the team agreed that training from within would also be crucial. The Nalu Surf management team identified the following two situations as circumstances where inside training would prove beneficial.

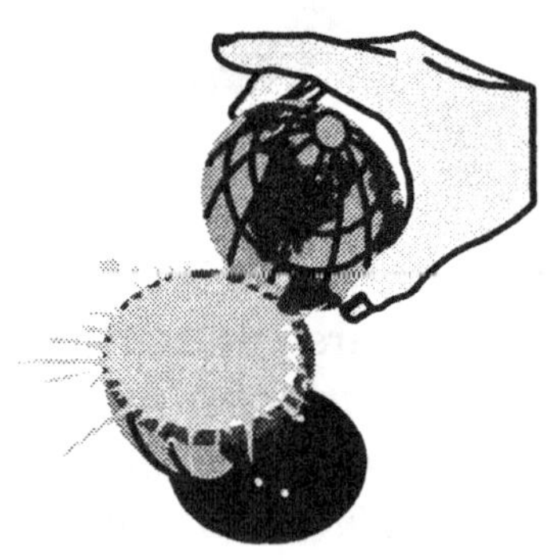

1. The toxic waste handling problem:

The senior management team felt that Andre, a line manager at Honolulu's manufacturing plant, could best handle this training, since he was the most knowledgeable about the requirements.

2. Declining sales at retail outlets:

The team decided that the managers at each outlet could best handle each particular situation, since they knew their salespeople better than anyone else. For example, Raylene, the manager at the Los Angeles outlet, would be tasked with coaching her salespeople.

Both Andre and Raylene were familiar with the High-IMPACT Training Model, since it was covered in the corporate training course that all managers attend. In fact, Raylene had previously used the model for training new employees. Andre, a new employee, had yet to apply his coaching and facilitating skills. Soon, both would be put to the test.

Getting Ready For Training

As you've already learned, there are plenty of things to do before you actually begin training. You certainly wouldn't gather your group together or plop down in front of the individual you're training and say, *"All right, let's begin. Now, what am I supposed to teach you?!"* You've got to do your homework first. Good coaches and facilitators *prepare.* Your students shouldn't be guinea pigs who *may* learn something if they're lucky!

I Phase One: Identifying Training Needs

Competent coaches and facilitators first determine what exactly needs to be learned. Why go into excruciating detail over how to use a software package if your organization doesn't require its employees to know that skill? Or maybe the skill is important, but half of the individuals in your group already know 75 percent of what you're explaining. They may tune out your whole message because they're bored, or they don't feel the skill is important for their jobs, or they believe you're only going to cover information they already know.

Identifying training needs means considering the requirements of your organization, your organization's customers, and the needs of the individuals you are going to coach. The process gives you the answers to important questions, such as:

- ✧ In broad terms, what is the performance problem?
- ✧ Who specifically needs the training?
- ✧ What performance is expected from your staff to meet customer and organizational needs?
- ✧ Will training actually help those performance problems go away? Or, are the problems a result of other circumstances that need attention, such as outdated work tools, inappropriate compensation programs, safety concerns, and so forth?
- ✧ What content should I cover? Do I need to deal with attitudes, skills, and/or knowledge?
- ✧ When I finish, what specific changes in performance should I expect to see after the training?

If you accurately identify training needs, your training will be targeted correctly, and you'll be ready to plan an instructional approach that will actually improve job performance. It's the first step in effective training, and a critical prerequisite for successful coaches and facilitators.

In Honolulu...

Andre, the newly hired line manager at Nalu Surf's manufacturing plant, investigated the toxic waste handling problem. Once he'd studied the legal requirements for handling toxins, he clearly identified problems that were resulting from improper handling. Then, he formulated a list of the correct procedures to follow. After this, he observed the work force in action to see where the gaps in performance were occurring. Of the twelve men who were involved with the handling of toxic waste, he was surprised to find that four weren't performing the required steps....

In Los Angeles...

Raylene, the manager at Nalu Surf's retail store, looked into the gaps in performance of her salespeople: late to work, taking too much time with custom orders, sales quotas not being met, etc. The twenty salespeople under her command, both part- and full-timers, all showed varying signs of decreasing performance. Something definitely had to be done. . . .

Phase Two: Map The Approach

Once you've identified the gaps between expected and actual performance, it's time to focus more closely on your target audience. You've identified who needs coaching and facilitating in general; now's your chance to put your potential *trainees* under your microscope of assessment. Observe them, meet with them, and question them. Your goal is to determine what kind of training will bring their performance up to par, given their current attitudes, skills, and knowledge.

Maybe your organization has purchased a new, automated phone answering system that all customer service representatives must learn. Suddenly, the job description for customer service representatives changes to include mastery of the new tool. In Phase One, you have identified the exact skills they need to master. In this phase, you'll determine the best approach to training this particular group. Perhaps you'll choose a hands-on, two-day seminar with quick-reference job aids, and supplemental peer coaching in the weeks that follow.

In Honolulu...

Andre observed and met with the four workers who were incorrectly handling toxic waste. It became clear that they weren't aware of all of the procedures, were sometimes just plain sloppy, frequently didn't take the time to follow the procedures completely, or a combination of these factors. His training, then, was more complicated than he first thought. It would have to address knowledge, skills, *and* attitudes. Andre decided that facilitating a small group session with visual aids and handouts would be helpful first, after which he would coach the men one-on-one to ensure success....

In Los Angeles...

Raylene knew the training job ahead of her was immense; but, putting it off would only result in diminishing profits for Nalu Surf and a negative performance review for her. She sorted out the various gaps in performance and discovered that the time her salespeople spent with customers on custom orders could be reduced with improved sales techniques. For example, most of the salespeople wandered around the store with customers, leisurely exchanging surf stories, and occasionally pointing out various features on several stock surfboards, only to discover that the customer was actually seeking a custom-made board.

Raylene, along with her assistant manager, Max, decided that they could streamline the sales process and that training would not be effective until this took place. Together, they created a list of probing questions that their sales staff could ask customers to quickly determine needs. In addition, they designed a worksheet that would help customers design a custom board to fit their requirements. Only after the process was changed were they ready to think about coaching their sales force.

Raylene and Max chose to introduce the new question list and worksheet at a series of brief Saturday group sessions. Since many of their employees attended school, this appeared to be the best choice. Raylene also videotaped Max in role-play scenarios, questioning customers and helping them complete worksheets, so the employees could see the process modeled on tape....

Phase Three: Produce Learning Tools

After you've mapped your approach, it's time to produce learning tools to help in your presentation of the material you need to cover. Training support materials can greatly enhance your coaching and facilitating. They include overhead transparencies, flip charts, films, videotapes, audiotapes, handouts, job aids, practice scenarios, and so forth. You may even have the time and resources to create learning tools using advanced computer and video technology. These program materials help maximize learning, but require careful, up-front planning and development.

Coaches and facilitators use support materials to introduce and clarify key points, to strengthen and reinforce participant understanding, and to increase attention and retention by participants. Preparing these materials will also focus your attention on what lies ahead—the actual coaching and facilitating process.

In Honolulu...

Andre spent several busy days in preparation for his coaching sessions. He decided to preview and purchase a videotape on the dangers of handling toxins in the surfboard manufacturing industry, and prepared flip charts and handouts covering the major procedural guidelines for dealing with toxins.

In Los Angeles...

Raylene and Max spent hours in their preparation of materials. First, they teamed with their best salespeople to create the probing questions *"cheat sheet"* list. Then, they produced an easy-to-use surfboard-design worksheet and refined it with the help of some frequent customers and board shapers. They had all of the materials professionally printed and included them in a small training binder.

Raylene then checked out the company's VHS video camera from the regional office, and taped Max performing the skills she wanted to cover in the training.

Raylene also prepared overhead transparencies of the question list and the custom worksheet. She also wrote some typical role-play scenarios for practice in the sessions.

Chapter Six Worksheet: Planning For Success

Consider a potential training need within your organization and complete these plans:

1. Identify training needs.

a. Briefly describe the performance problem.

b. Who needs the training?

c. What performance standards do you expect the employees to meet?

d. Could training really solve the problem?

e. What content should you cover?

f. What performance improvements do you expect to see after the training?

2. Map your approach. What type of training would be best, given the content and the trainee audience? Explain why you've chosen each component of the design.

3. Produce your learning tools. What obstacles might you face in developing your learning tools, and how might you overcome them?

Employing Successful Delivery Skills

All the preparation in the world won't help if you can't adequately express your ideas, thoughts, and feelings. The delivery of training materials can be a very difficult experience for a non-trainer, and is certainly a demanding one for a novice. Even professionals continually seek to improve upon their presentation skills.

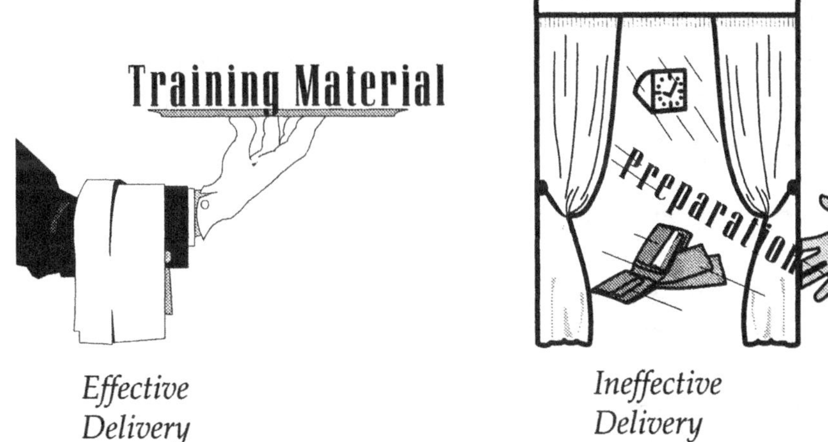

Effective Delivery

Ineffective Delivery

Think of your presentation skills as a key medium through which learning occurs. Your focus can be exactly on target, your materials tremendous, and your training design excellent, but if you can't pull off the delivery effectively, you're throwing all your preparation, time, and money out the window. It's essentially the difference between handing the training material to your participants on a silver platter or tossing all of your preparation out the window. You can make learning easy or virtually inaccessible.

To enhance communication of the materials, you must skillfully incorporate a variety of delivery skills *(both verbal and nonverbal).* Your goal is to facilitate learning, not to bore, alienate, or ignore the individuals you're coaching! Therefore, coaches and facilitators must learn to be aware of not only *what* content they are delivering, but also *how* they are delivering it.

Verbal Delivery Skills

One of your greatest tools as a coach and facilitator is your voice. To use your voice to its best advantage, you should attempt to develop a voice that incorporates the following characteristics:

Pleasant—A pleasant voice conveys a sense a warmth and is easy to listen to over extended periods of time. If you're coaching one-on-one or in small groups, a pleasant voice is an especially important commodity.

Natural—A voice that is natural reflects your true personality and sincerity. It doesn't come across to others as being *"practiced"* or *"constrained."* In addition, use a natural, even pace—not too fast, not too slow.

Dynamic—A dynamic voice gives the impression of force and strength, even when it isn't especially loud. It commands attention at appropriate times. It's helpful to develop a dynamic voice for speaking in front of large groups.

Expressive—An expressive voice portrays various shades of meaning. It never sounds monotonous or emotionless.

Easily Heard—If your voice can be easily heard, it projects the proper volume for the size of the group to whom you're speaking. Also, making sure you are easily heard is especially important when using AV equipment or darkening the room. Some trainers speak too loudly or softly, which turns off listeners.

Each of these characteristics of an effective speaking voice is vital to your success as a coach and facilitator. To illustrate this point, consider a speaker whose voice has none of these characteristics. The voice has nasal undertones, becomes unnaturally high at certain intervals, is not dynamic or expressive, and is either too loud or too soft. It's doubtful you'll remember much of what is said!

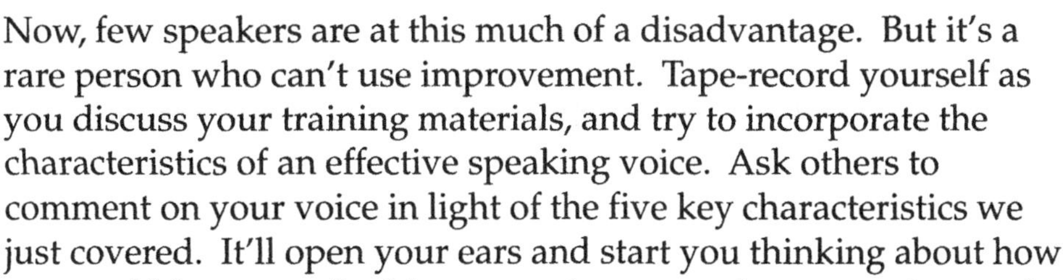

Now, few speakers are at this much of a disadvantage. But it's a rare person who can't use improvement. Tape-record yourself as you discuss your training materials, and try to incorporate the characteristics of an effective speaking voice. Ask others to comment on your voice in light of the five key characteristics we just covered. It'll open your ears and start you thinking about how you could improve. In this case, as in many others, practice results in improved performance.

In Honolulu...

Andre had his training materials prepared and ready. Since this was his first coaching opportunity at Nalu Surf, he wanted to perform well. He tape-recorded himself practicing his opening comments to the team. While his voice sounded pleasant enough, it seemed a little forced, and he thought he was coming across as though he was irritated. He took a deep breath and tried again....

In Los Angeles...

Raylene and Max practiced portions of their session in front of each other. Raylene decided that Max was a more dynamic speaker, so he would begin the session. But she was determined to improve....

Nonverbal Delivery Skills

While you're conducting a coaching session, you can use more than your voice as an effective tool. Using your body is also an effective means to add emphasis and clarity to your words. It can be your most powerful tool for convincing participants of your sincerity, depth of knowledge, confidence, and enthusiasm.

Presentation form and style involve the whole person. When you are coaching or facilitating, individuals pick up visual messages in your posture, hand gestures, body movements, facial expressions, and eye contact. If you desire to become a successful coach and facilitator, it is essential that you understand how your body speaks. You can't prevent sending nonverbal messages, but you certainly can learn to manage and control them.

Each of the major characteristics that communicates a visual message to individuals can be further described as follows:

Posture

Your posture reflects your attitude. It conveys to your listeners whether or not you are confident, alert, enthusiastic, and in command of yourself and your coaching/facilitating session. If you are speaking to a large group, stand tall and confidently. If you are seated while coaching an individual or small group, sit up straight. Changing your posture to reflect confidence often requires little more than remembering to do so.

Hand gestures

A hand gesture is a specific movement that reinforces a verbal message or conveys a particular thought or emotion. Gestures made above the shoulder level tend to suggest physical height, inspiration, or emotional excitement. Gestures made below waist level tend to suggest rejection, apathy, or condemnation. Those made between the waist and shoulder level tend to suggest calmness and serenity. To use gestures effectively:

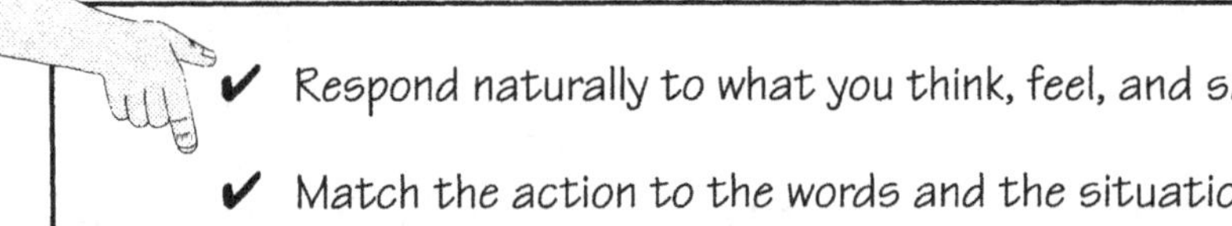

- ✔ Respond naturally to what you think, feel, and say
- ✔ Match the action to the words and the situation
- ✔ Use gestures that are pleasing and convincing
- ✔ Ensure that your gestures are smooth and well-timed

Body movements

Changing your position or physical location while presenting information communicates a message *(intentional or otherwise)* to the individuals you're coaching. The key point to remember about body movement is to *"never move without a reason."* The eye is inevitably attracted to a moving object, so any full-body movements you make during a coaching session invite attention. Take these body movement tips into consideration:

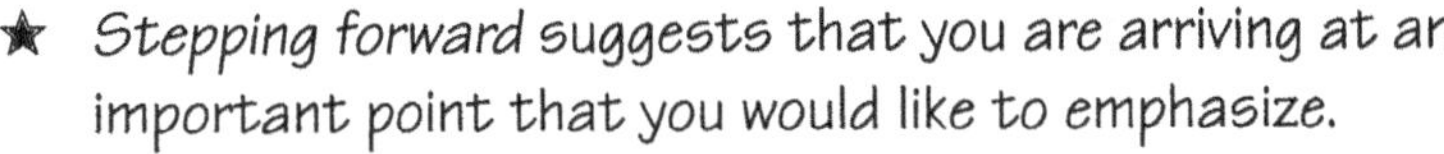

★ *Stepping forward* suggests that you are arriving at an important point that you would like to emphasize.

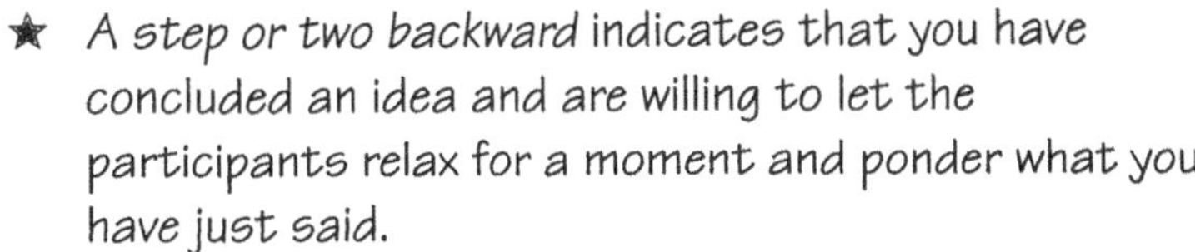

★ *A step or two backward* indicates that you have concluded an idea and are willing to let the participants relax for a moment and ponder what you have just said.

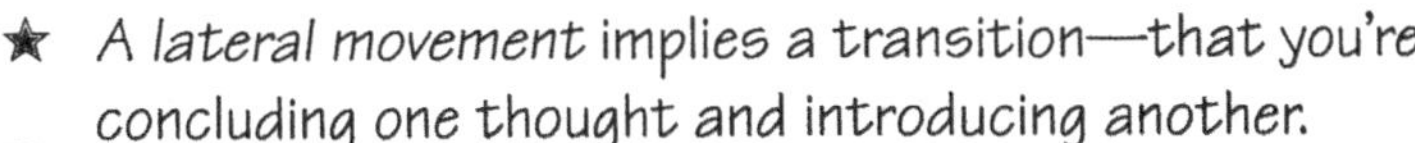

★ *A lateral movement* implies a transition—that you're concluding one thought and introducing another.

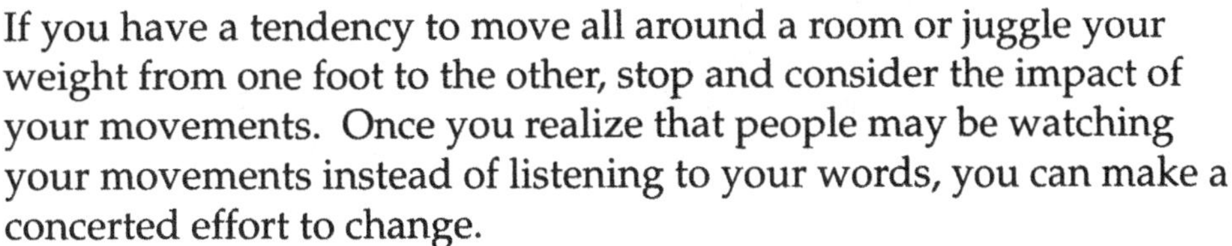

If you have a tendency to move all around a room or juggle your weight from one foot to the other, stop and consider the impact of your movements. Once you realize that people may be watching your movements instead of listening to your words, you can make a concerted effort to change.

All of this information also applies if you're coaching an individual or small group while seated. Your hand movements are comparable to the body movements of standing facilitators. Seated coaches may unconsciously fidget with items, touch various parts of their faces, or crack their knuckles. Become more conscious of your hands if you're seated. Don't let them become the focus of your participants' attention!

Facial expressions

Participants typically watch a trainer's face during a session. Politeness, of course, may be one reason for this. Equally important, however, is an individual's need to obtain visual, *"facial expression"* feedback from the facilitator that will help make the message more meaningful and understandable.

The individuals involved in a coaching session want the facilitator to be confident, friendly, and sincere. In fact, they will often look to your face for evidence of these qualities. Strange as it sounds, the first step toward projecting these qualities is to recognize expressions that don't belong on your face.

Possible solutions to minimize unnatural facial expressions include:

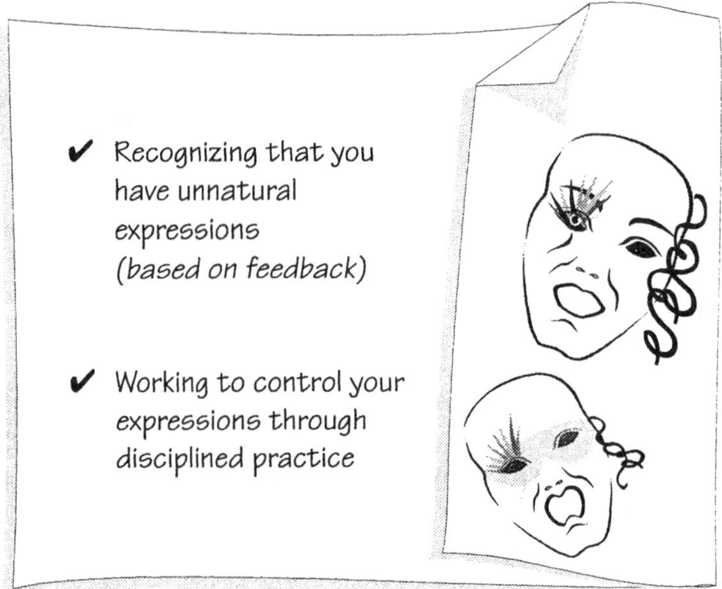

Thorough preparation and knowledge of your material will help you project confidence and control through your body motions and facial expressions.

Eye contact

Eye contact is the cohesive element that bonds coaches with the individuals they're training. When conducting a coaching session, you can use your eyes to interest and involve participants. Several strategies for establishing effective eye contact include:

Know your material

You should prepare and rehearse program content to the point where you don't have to look frequently at notes.

Establish rapport with the participants

Making effective eye contact means more than just passing your gaze over the room or around the table; it means focusing your eyes for a few seconds on individual participants throughout the session, and building person-to-person relationships with them. If you're coaching an individual, your frequent eye contact with that person is vitally important.

Monitor visual feedback

When you're in a coaching session, individuals respond with their own nonverbal feedback. Use your eyes to actively seek out this feedback. By monitoring these visual messages, you can gauge the group's reactions *(or an individual's reaction, if in a one-on-one situation)* to what you say, then adjust your presentation accordingly.

As with verbal delivery skills, assessment and practice of nonverbal behaviors are vital to your success. For these nonverbal skills, a videotape of your practice or of your performance in an actual coaching situation will provide you with invaluable information. Practice more, then videotape again. Continue this process until you're confident that your nonverbal delivery skills will enhance, rather than detract from, your well-prepared materials.

In Honolulu...

Andre asked another line manager, Greg, to videotape his first coaching session. *"It's not to put you on the spot,"* Andre explained to the four men present. *"I'm new at this coaching and want to see how I can improve."*

Looking at the videotape later that night, Andre noticed that whenever one of the men asked him a question, he'd frown and look off into the distance. Although it was just his way of concentrating, Andre sensed a negative response to the nonverbal expression. In addition, his voice was still communicating an *"irritated"* attitude. He noted it and resolved to practice ways to alter the frown on his face and eliminate the *"frown"* in his voice.

In Los Angeles...

Raylene asked Max to rate her while she practiced her nonverbal delivery skills. *"And I'll rate you,"* she said. *"But we have to be honest. Otherwise, there's no purpose in it."* Each started the critiquing session by emphasizing the positive. Max pointed out Raylene's effective eye contact and good posture. *"What you might consider working on,"* he suggested, *"are your hand gestures. You tend to wave your hands around a lot. It's quite distracting."*

Raylene nodded. *"I've always known that my hands are too expressive. You'll have to help me on that one, especially since your gesturing works well. You come across as very confident."* She paused and thought for a moment. *"I think you'd do best to work on eye contact. You looked above me, instead of at me. But that's an easy one to improve."*

Mastering verbal and nonverbal delivery skills will earn you above-average scores in successful coaching and facilitating. Showing competence in the skills outlined in the next chapter, *"Using Support Materials Effectively,"* edges that score even higher.

Chapter Seven Worksheet: Assessing Your Delivery

You should continually assess your delivery skills. Have someone videotape you conducting a real or practice training session; then rate yourself on this worksheet after watching the videotape. If you don't have a videotape recorder, ask an observer to rate you on the following skills during the above session.

Circle a rating of 1 to 5 *(a 5 is an excellent rating; a 1 refers to "needing much improvement")* for each of the skills.

1. Verbal Delivery Skills
Rate the following skills that apply to vocal quality:

a. pleasant	1	2	3	4	5
b. natural	1	2	3	4	5
c. dynamic	1	2	3	4	5
d. expressive	1	2	3	4	5
e. easily heard	1	2	3	4	5

2. Nonverbal Delivery Skills
Rate the following skills that apply to visual communication:

a. posture	1	2	3	4	5
b. hand gestures	1	2	3	4	5
c. body movements	1	2	3	4	5
d. facial expressions	1	2	3	4	5
e. eye contact	1	2	3	4	5

3. Choose one of your lowest-rated verbal delivery skills. How can you improve that skill?

4. Choose one of your lowest-rated nonverbal delivery skills. Why is it an important skill? How can you improve it?

USING SUPPORT MATERIALS EFFECTIVELY

You have tremendous materials planned for your coaching session. You're employing successful delivery skills, impressing the participants by presenting your knowledge in an articulate and confident manner. You're on a high, stimulated by the enthusiastic response of the group you're coaching. And then it happens. You didn't have time to check your photocopied handouts, and a critical page is missing. Then the bulb burns out in the overhead projector. Finally, the video you chose is jittery on the screen and you can't seem to adjust it. Individuals start mumbling and moving about in their seats. Your presentation nosedives.

An uncommon scenario? You might like to think so, but it's not out-of-the-ordinary. Support materials and equipment can be an excellent adjunct to your presentation, but you have to use them effectively. The success of your performance doesn't hinge only on your verbal and nonverbal delivery skills. You must also use your program materials competently, so they'll enhance the learning even further.

Characteristics Of High-IMPACT Program Materials

High-IMPACT program materials can add substantially to your program. But what exactly constitutes High-IMPACT materials? To identify and consequently develop High-IMPACT materials, look for the following *"quality indicators."*

Utilizing quality indicators will help ensure your program materials' effectiveness. High-IMPACT program materials are:

Visible

Your support materials need to be easily seen by all the individuals you are coaching. If your group is large, this will be more of a challenge. A group of thirty individuals scattered around a room may have a difficult time seeing a flip chart page on which you've listed fifteen items. If you want to use the flip chart, consider listing three or four items per page in large print. Information that can't be seen is worthless and frustrating to participants.

Simple

Try not to present too much information on one visual. The content of your material should be easily digestible; therefore, limit the amount of information you include. Make use of key words and concepts, instead of full sentences or paragraphs. High-IMPACT materials keep it simple so individuals can easily remember what you want them to.

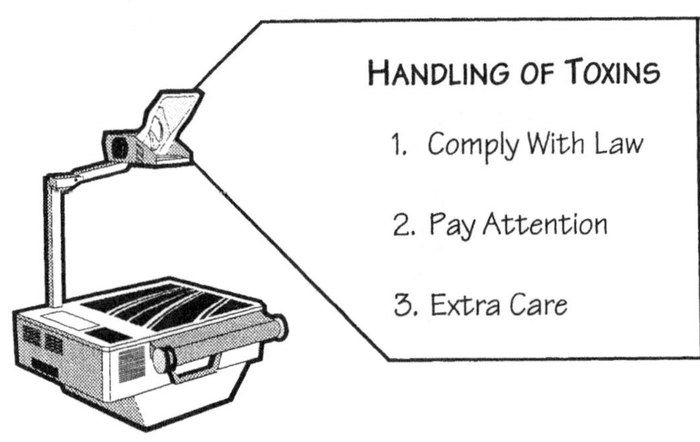

Accurate

Present information that is up-to-date and factual. If you show an outdated videotape to individuals you're coaching, they may feel that everything you're teaching them is useless. Ditto with incorrect information. It could have an extremely negative impact on your coaching.

If you've used your training materials previously, and you're revising them, make sure those revisions are reflected in all of your support materials. For example, if you're illustrating a process that you've amended to include an extra step, correct all of your support materials to reflect the change—including overheads, handouts, job aids, flip charts, and so forth.

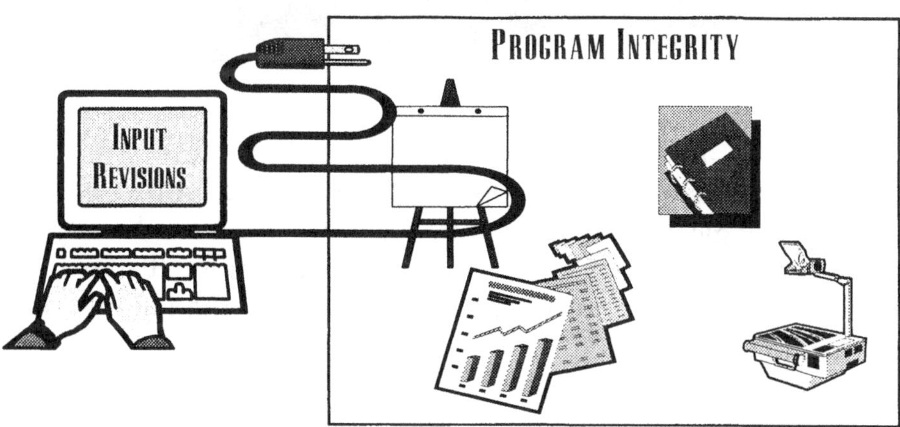

Interesting

This characteristic of High-IMPACT program materials is especially important to adult learners. They've been through the boring history films in school and painfully recall sleeping through slide presentations on verb conjugations. Don't count on support materials to command your participants' attention just because they deviate from the lecture mode. Make them interesting by using colors, overlays, and illustrations. Arrange the information in a creative way to help develop and maintain attention.

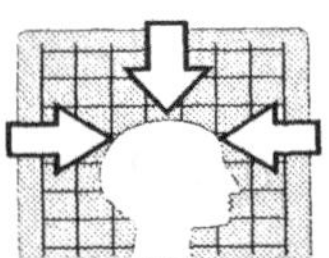

Practical

This characteristic also applies to the adult learning principles. You have to gear your program materials to the individuals you are coaching. Your program materials have to be *"easily identified with"* from the participants' point of view. For example, if you're including an analogy in one of your materials, make it one to which your participants can relate.

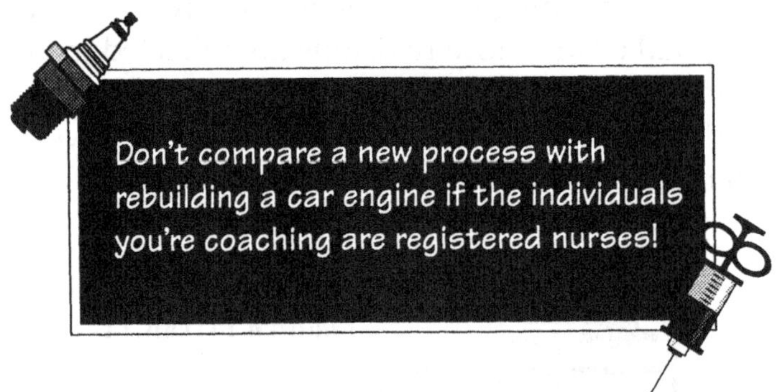

If your program materials exhibit these quality indicators, you can be assured that the individual you're coaching or the group you're facilitating will glean more from your presentation. Include only High-IMPACT program materials in your presentation. It's far better to have a few High-IMPACT materials rather than many ineffectual ones.

In Honolulu...

Andre knew that his choice of a toxins-handling video would have to be discerning. After all, it had to appeal to four beefy line workers who wouldn't put up with *"rinky-dink visuals."* He liked one he previewed from a surfers' environmental group, because it was interesting, current, and informative. Watching the video left one in no doubt as to the danger of shaping polystyrene foam blanks, inhaling polystyrene vapor and urethane, and disposing of strong solvents—all substances his men worked with....

In Los Angeles...

Raylene and Max worked together, editing their role-modeling video, and prepared overhead transparencies of their *"probing question"* lists, custom surfboard worksheets, and practice scenarios. Max drew cartoons that illustrated the major points on the overheads, and they assembled the trainee notebooks....

Determining which High-IMPACT program materials to use and creating them is only half the battle. You also have to use them effectively. If you don't, your High-IMPACT materials suddenly turn into low or negative-impact materials. And that's exactly what you don't want to happen. The good news is that it's preventable. Just learn to use your support materials effectively by mastering the following guidelines.

Guidelines For Use

These guidelines will help you expand your coaching effectiveness, which translates into increased learning and improved job performance for the individuals you are coaching.

Flip Chart

- Write rapidly and legibly; don't be afraid to misspell or abbreviate words as you write quickly in class.
- Talk as you write and face the audience when possible. *(Don't hesitate to ask for assistance in turning pages or writing.)*
- Use color *(and/or a pencil or pen as a pointer)* to retain attention.
- Tear off sheets and post them around the room when appropriate, using masking tape only *(other tape can damage walls).*
- Use symbols, circles, different colors, and underlines to help separate ideas and highlight key concepts.

Overhead Transparencies

- Check that the overhead projector has an extra bulb and that you know how to replace it.
- Avoid becoming a part of the transparency (*e.g., having a portion of the overhead projection appear on you, etc.*).
- Use your pencil as a pointer to emphasize detail.
- Use a sheet of paper to allow you to reveal a portion of the transparency while temporarily blocking out the rest.
- Demonstrate how to complete an actual sample form with the group using overhead pens. Overlay one on another to show a diagram developed in sequence, a completed worksheet, or an evolving flow chart.

Slides

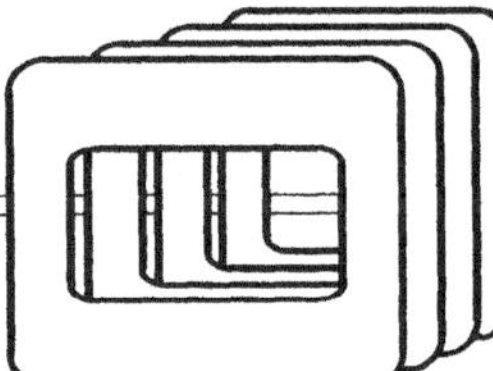

- Preview the slides shortly before the session to ensure they are ready to use (*none upside down or backward*) when you need them.
- Follow your presentation plan, sharing pre-rehearsed key points for each slide.
- Speak with more volume than you normally use. (*As with other media, the listener's attention is divided; in a darkened room, more volume will help hold attention.*)
- Use a remote control to allow you to move during the training.
- Vary the pace of slides being presented, making sure to not "flash" too quickly or "hold" for too long. (*An average = 15-20 seconds per slide.*) Also, break the presentation into short segments of 5 or 6 slides, if possible.

Print Materials

- ✰ Familiarize yourself with the print materials before distributing them to the learners.
- ✰ Use a highlighter to mark key points you will want to share with the participants.
- ✰ Point out how information is structured so that the content is easily accessible.
- ✰ Provide reproducibles for on-the-job use.
- ✰ Distribute print materials at appropriate times:

Print Materials	Before	During	After
• An outline	Great	No	Okay
• Material critical to the discussion	Great	Okay	No
• A summary or synopsis	Okay	No	Great
• Additional support materials (*e.g., Reproducible Masters*)	No	Okay	Great

Video

- ✰ Preview the video again just prior to using it in a training situation.
- ✰ *"Cue"* videos so they are *"ready to roll"* when used, rather than causing the participants to view several minutes of blank screen.
- ✰ Provide a level of lighting that allows participants to take notes if they wish.
- ✰ Play the video at an appropriate volume.
- ✰ Pause the video during opportune points to encourage discussion —an excellent way to actively involve participants.

In Honolulu...

In his training session, Andre was ready to show the video of the dangers of toxic waste. He had it cued to roll immediately. As the screen flashed the title, the background music blared so loudly that everyone jumped. Andre quickly turned the volume down. *"Uh-oh,"* he thought to himself. *"That's something I should have checked beforehand."*

In Los Angeles...

The overhead transparencies went over well during the first session. Raylene demonstrated for the salespeople how to help customers fill out the custom-board worksheet step-by-step. She blocked off the steps on the transparency she had yet to discuss with a piece of paper, then revealed each step as she explained it. The group was in an uproar over Max's cartoons that accompanied each probing sales question.

Using your support materials effectively will help your training experience run more smoothly. For further techniques that will enhance your coaching and facilitating skills, read on.

Chapter Eight Worksheet: Improving Program Materials And Their Use

Consider a recent experience as either a participant or a leader in a training session and please respond to the following:

1. List two examples of trainer support materials that were not designed or produced to be effective.

2. How could the materials in Question # 1 have been designed to be more effective?

3. List two examples of trainer support materials that were not used properly, regardless of an effective design.

4. How could the materials in Question # 3 have been effectively presented?

Enhancing Coaching/ Facilitating Skills

Having a good grasp of delivery skills and being able to use support materials effectively both contribute to a successful coaching experience. To be a truly effective facilitator, however, you must also know how to field questions, arrange rooms for impact, and handle challenging participant behaviors.

Fielding Questions

Occasionally, even the most experienced coaches and facilitators are concerned when they're hit with situations like the following:

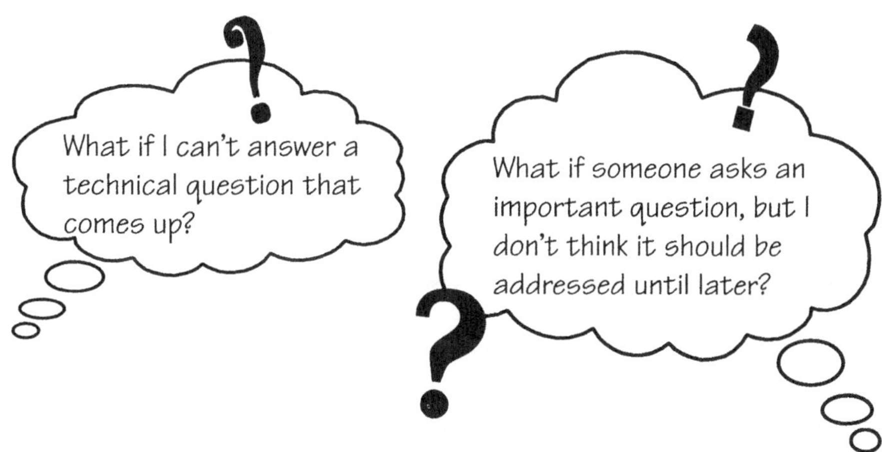

As an effective coach and facilitator, you'll invite questions during your coaching session. Handling them during the session encourages participation, provides a feel for audience acceptance, and enables you to correct information or enhance discussion. On the other hand, handling questions during the session may negatively impact time schedules and program continuity if not handled appropriately.

Your ability to field questions effectively can make or break a coaching session. The following suggestions should prove helpful in fielding questions.

Repeat or rephrase the question

If you repeat or rephrase a question, you will ensure that all participants hear it *(if you're facilitating learning within a group).* It also buys you additional time to think about a possible way to respond, and an opportunity to restate the question *(if necessary)* in more favorable terms. For example, suppose an individual asks,

You can respond by rephrasing the question as a statement:

You can then defuse a potential problem situation by stating some facts about the situation, and directing the answer away from your own opinion *(which may inflame the situation even more).*

Receive all questions cordially

You should always remain courteous and agreeable. Don't get ruffled by negative or hostile remarks. Maintaining your composure is key to effectively fielding questions.

Evaluate the relevance of the question

If the question is relevant, respond accordingly. If not, or if the response is relevant only to the questioner, consider giving a brief explanation, then inviting the participant to speak with you privately after the session. If you're coaching one-on-one and the question isn't relevant to what you're currently covering, write the question down and inform your trainee that you'll get to it later. That way he knows you consider the question important.

Always address a question

As much as you'd like to pretend you didn't hear a question you don't know the answer to, don't. You need to address every question. Just respond with,

Then, make sure you follow-up with that individual or group.

Be brief

It's not good practice to break the continuity of a presentation with lengthy answers. Be as brief as you can while still providing a complete answer that is acceptable to the questioner. When you ask those you are coaching if there are further questions and there are none, it's also helpful to make a summarizing statement and move on.

In Honolulu...

Andre started a discussion after the video on toxic waste. Bill, one of the workers who had sat through the video with his arms folded, interrupted Andre with, *"Come on, boss...how the h- - - are we supposed to follow those procedures when we don't even have time to go to the bathroom!"* Andre swallowed hard and paused. *"That's a very relevant question,"* he began, then continued with a response that focused on the dangerous effects of not adhering to the process. Andre could have risen to Bill's bait with a smart remark, but his cordial answer kept Bill's attention....

In Los Angeles...

The sales personnel had many questions. A couple of them focused on whether or not they should still talk about the size of the surf and weather conditions with customers as a means of building rapport. *"Listen, I think it's great that you talk surf with customers, but we've got to move as quickly as possible toward finding out what they're looking for,"* said Max. *"You can build rapport even better by getting the details about what kind of board will really meet their needs. That's what brings a customer back!"* The group acquiesced....

Again, practice is the only way you'll learn to effectively field questions. And, in this instance, the actual coaching/facilitating session is the best practice ground. You can have a colleague question you about the content of your presentation, but it's in the context of the actual situation that you'll be able to test your ability to deal with individuals who ask challenging or irrelevant questions. Being prepared for that possibility and having a plan ready for action will definitely enhance your coaching/facilitating skills.

Arranging Rooms For Impact

The seating arrangement of the room in which you're coaching or facilitating will be determined to a great extent by the type of training you're doing. If your presentation involves a lot of small group interaction, for example, you wouldn't want to facilitate learning in a work area filled with cubicles.

Keep the following tips in mind as you consider arranging your room for the best impact:

1. Typically, it's best to have those you're coaching feel that they are an active part of the training.
2. You will be more effective at presenting content if you do not stand behind an obstruction during the presentation (e.g., lectern, table, machinery, etc.).
3. Allocate an appropriate number of chairs—let the individuals you're coaching have room to sit. Remember, they may be there for several hours.
4. Avoid arranging tables and chairs so close together that neither you nor your participants can move freely around them.

In Honolulu...

Andre decided that a circle of five chairs for him and the men would work best for his presentation. The close contact should involve the men more and keep them focused on the material, and the men could easily shift their chairs around to view the video....

In Los Angeles...

Raylene and Max arranged chairs in the large storage room for their sales force. Raylene thought that tables would be helpful, but there wasn't enough room to move around them easily, so she and Max bought clipboards for each salesperson. That way they could write notes and practice filling out the worksheets....

Arranging your training room for impact is a relatively easy way to enhance your coaching/facilitating skills. Less easy is handling participants who seem determined to make the session more difficult for you and the other participants.

Handling Challenging Participants

Let's face it. Challenging participant behaviors will arise while you are coaching individuals and facilitating learning among groups. How you handle these situations will help determine your success as a coach and facilitator. The following guidelines will help you manage problem behaviors, should they arise. Note that many techniques may *"overlap"* to address other behaviors.

Behavior # 1: Highly argumentative or antagonistic

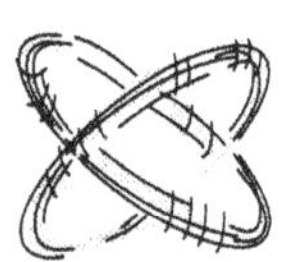

Individuals who come across as highly argumentative or antagonistic may have a combative personality. Or they may normally be good-natured, but have become upset by others' opinions. You may be dealing with show-offs, or individuals who lack the ability to state suggestions constructively. They may be antagonized over another issue, or upset because they're being ignored. Or, they may just be resistant to change, which is a common and natural reaction to some new concepts or skills covered in training.

Possible techniques to deal with this behavior:

- ☐ Control your own temper, and don't let the group (*if it's a group situation*) get excited either. Paraphrase the argumentative comments without using *"aggravating"* language.
- ☐ Respond to their content, not to their attack.
- ☐ Find merit in one of their points. Express your agreement, and then move on.
- ☐ Confront such individuals more directly and privately during a break. Try to find out what's irritating them.

Behavior # 2: Rambling

Ramblers often share information about everything except the topic at hand. They sometimes use farfetched analogies and steer the group or you off-track. The may also suffer from *"analysis paralysis"* and be afraid to make a decision.

Possible techniques to deal with this behavior:

- When you're dealing with ramblers, thank them for their comments when they stop to take a breath. Refocus their attention by restating the agenda, the relevant points, and the time limits. Move on.
- Ask them to clarify how their comments have expanded on the discussion at hand.
- Glance at your watch while they are speaking.

Behavior # 3: Overly talkative or dominant

These individuals may be *"eager beavers"* or show-offs, overly prepared, and/or have little self-confidence, and thus are *"overcompensating."* They may be well-informed and eager to show it, or may just naturally need attention. Dominant people may also have the most authority and enjoy captive audiences, or they simply may tend to be long-winded.

Possible techniques to deal with this behavior:

- Avoid embarrassing the participant or being sarcastic. It's not professional; besides, you may need their opinions later.
- Slow them down with a difficult question.
- Interject with: *"That's an interesting point. Let's see what the group thinks of it."*
- Use the rest of the group to cut a talker off (*e.g., "How do the rest of you feel about spending more time on this? Or should we move on?"*).
- Confront talkers gently during a break or after the session.

Behavior # 4: Having side conversations

Individuals who are involved in side conversations while you are in the midst of your presentation can be quite distracting to both you and other participants. These individuals may be discussing the subject at hand or having a completely different conversation, but in either circumstance, this behavior is disruptive.

Possible techniques to deal with this behavior:

- ☐ Call on one of the individuals by name, and ask him an easy question.
- ☐ Call on one by name, restate the last comment expressed by another participant (*or you*), and ask his opinion of it.
- ☐ Stand casually near the side conversationalists.

BLAH, BLAH

BLAH, BLAH, BLAH

Behavior # 5: Responding with an answer that's clearly wrong or off-track

It may take you off-guard when a participant shares an obviously wrong or irrelevant response during an open discussion. If you deal sensitively with this situation, however, it will earn you respect as an effective coach and facilitator.

Possible techniques to deal with this behavior:

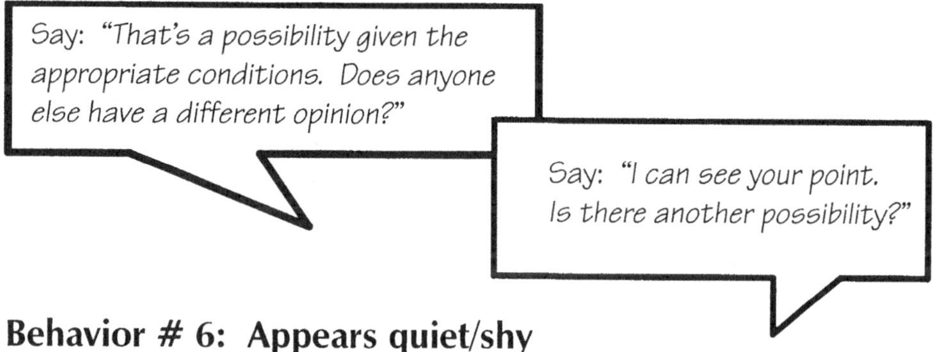

Behavior # 6: Appears quiet/shy

Participants who appear quiet or shy may be bored, indifferent, timid, or insecure. They may also come from a culture that doesn't encourage open, verbal participation in groups. In some situations, individuals who are quiet may actually feel superior and deem that it's not worthwhile to share their expertise with others. In other situations, a quiet person may actually be angry about having to attend the session.

Possible techniques to deal with this behavior:

- Don't ever force a person to express an opinion in a group.
- When you ask a question, make eye contact with those who appear quiet and/or shy.
- Involve quiet individuals in a small group activity, and ask them to report during the summary/debrief.
- Whenever they participate, recognize them sincerely.
- Mention to them during a break that you've noticed them being a bit "quiet" and ask for feedback.

Behavior # 7: Disagreeable

Disagreeable participants can put a kink in your presentation, especially if they adamantly disagree with you and the rest of the group *(if it's a group situation)* on a particular point.

Possible techniques to deal with this behavior:

- Throw the disagreeable participant's opinion out to the group. Give the group a chance to influence those who disagree.
- Mention that due to time constraints, you'd like to discuss it one-on-one later. Suggest they accept the majority opinion for the time being.
- Ask: *"What would it take for it to work for you?"*

In Honolulu...

Andre noticed that Mick, one of the men he was coaching, wasn't participating. Andre first tried to establish eye contact with him, but Mick kept looking down. When Andre asked the group to work through a problem-solving exercise, he asked Mick to report on the group's result. Mick agreed timidly, but without resistance. Mick's summary was brief and rather stilted, leading Andre to believe he was just shy. Andre thanked him for his contribution.

In Los Angeles...

Raylene noticed two of her salespeople talking among themselves when she was in the middle of a discussion of how to close sales. *"Jennifer,"* she began, *"the group seems to think that it's important to have a brief, informal conversation about surf conditions prior to discussing the type of board a customer might be looking for. What's your opinion about that?"* Jennifer stumbled a bit, agreed with the group, and refrained from side conversations for the rest of the session.

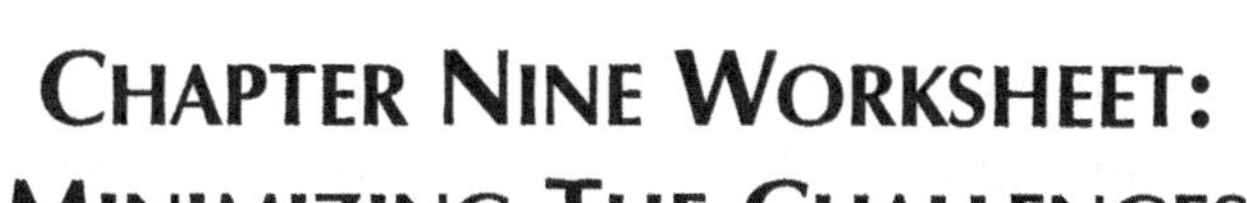

Chapter Nine Worksheet: Minimizing The Challenges

Some common challenges you may face when conducting coaching sessions are described below. For each, identify its potential cause(s), and two to three techniques you could use to minimize, control, or eliminate this challenge.

1. Tim's behavior during a recent training session has finally drawn complaints from other participants. When he participates in small and large group discussions, he dominates and discourages the others from contributing. When he has a question or comment, he blurts it out as an irritating interruption, without regard for the other participants. And when others offer opinions during discussions, he drives their ideas into the ground.

Potential causes:

____

____

____

____

Ways to minimize/control/eliminate:

____

____

____

____

2. You've just summarized the open discussion during a session, and for the third time, Judy has conveniently opted not to share any viewpoints or examples. During the break, you even overheard other participants complaining about her *"not carrying her load"* during small group activities, and they resent the fact that you're allowing her to get away with it. You've talked to her about this once before, she apologized, and that was that.

Possible cause(s):

Ways to minimize/control/eliminate:

3. Everything is set for your coaching session. You have participant materials, a full room of people, and fresh-brewed coffee. *What more could you ask for?* As you begin to lead an open discussion, you get blank stares. No one seems to want to talk, share an opinion or idea, or even ask a question. *The silence is deafening!* You can hear the coffee *(and your emotions)* brew.

Potential cause(s):

____

____

____

____

____

Ways to minimize/control/eliminate:

____

____

____

____

____

____

____

____

Tips For Different Situations

As a coach and facilitator, you'll encounter many different situations where you'll have to use your skills appropriately. While all situations require competent delivery skills, effective use of support materials, a carefully arranged room, and the ability to field questions and handle challenging behaviors, you'll use those skills to different degrees depending upon the situation. A one-on-one coaching session, for example, utilizes different instructional skills from large-group facilitation. This chapter takes a look at the two primary training experiences—one-on-one coaching and group facilitation—and provides tips for each.

One-On-One Coaching

A one-on-one coaching situation presents specific challenges and great opportunities. If you're not a professional trainer, the majority of your training experiences will be one-on-one. And yet, one-on-one coaching is often taken lightly. How frequently do you sweat over training an individual? It's usually the worries over group facilitating that keep you up the night before!

Because one-on-one training is not usually intimidating, you might tend to skip over some of the necessary planning. Don't. Planning is essential to a successful training session, and critical to the employee's success on the job. And in a one-on-one coaching situation, it's easier than you think. You have only one person to observe, only one person at whom your training will be targeted.

Establishing rapport is especially important at this point. You can make only one first impression. Establishing rapport is the process of getting on the correct wavelength with people.

Establishing rapport leads to mutual understanding and agreement. For this reason, it is a vital ingredient in the development of good working relationships. There are five key types of behavior in the creation of rapport:

Small Talk

Small talk can be used to establish shared experiences. Find something to share before getting down to business: it may be about the weather, or last night's game...the whole idea is to select a "*safe*" topic where the trainee will have no trouble meeting you halfway.

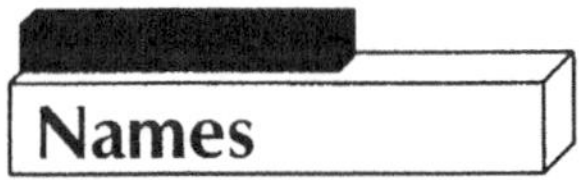

Names

Using a trainee's name frequently will help establish rapport as long as it is not inappropriately familiar or done in a routine, mechanical way.

Humor

If you can share something to laugh about, the way will be paved for a harmonious transaction. One technique for doing this is to make an amusing remark about yourself.

Empathy

Empathy is the ability to put yourself in the other person's shoes and see the situation from his/her point of view. Remember to *demonstrate* empathy, not just feel it. It is often confused with sympathy, but is fundamentally different. Sympathy means sharing the other person's feelings and emotions. Empathy means understanding.

Body Language

Nonverbal behavior also plays a key part. There is evidence to suggest that nonverbal behavior plays a greater role than anything else when establishing rapport. Apply the behaviors you've learned in this guidebook and you should do fine.

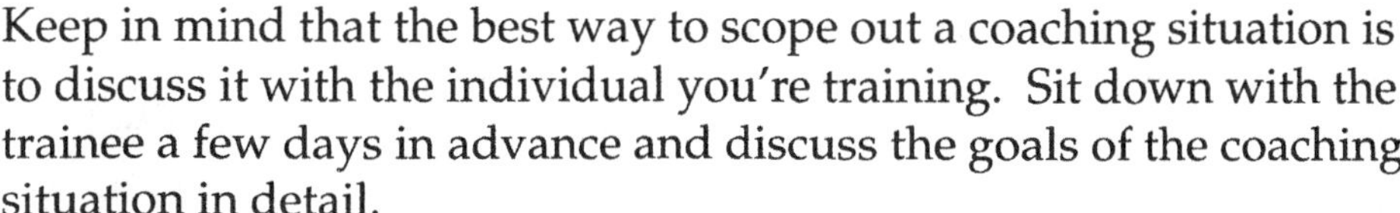

Keep in mind that the best way to scope out a coaching situation is to discuss it with the individual you're training. Sit down with the trainee a few days in advance and discuss the goals of the coaching situation in detail.

If you're coaching a new employee who is starting immediately, make this the first item on your agenda. Ask her what she hopes to learn, check to see if her specific goals mesh with yours, and discover where her strengths and weaknesses lie. If you're candid and upfront with her, most likely she'll respond accordingly. Keep in mind that while a new employee may not know much about her new training requirements, almost all current employees have well-reasoned opinions about their own training needs.

In this pre-coaching session, ask open-ended questions that can't be answered with a mere *"yes"* or *"no."* For example, ask questions such as these:

- ☐ From your perspective, what job tasks are you supposed to do each day?
- ☐ Which tasks are more difficult for you than others?
- ☐ In which job areas would training help you?
- ☐ Which training formats work best for you?

This initial session provides an ideal opportunity to learn about your trainee's learning style. Is she an individual who learns best through reading about a new procedure, and then experimenting with the equipment at her own pace? Or is expert demonstration, then hands-on practice the quickest way she'll master the new equipment? One-on-one coaching allows you to target your trainee's individual learning preferences so you'll both experience success.

Your verbal and nonverbal delivery skills will come in handy. Considering the close quarters of a one-on-one coaching situation, the importance of your nonverbal skills will be heightened. You'll need to tone down your gestures *(sweeping hand movements may knock your trainee in the nose!)*, and you'll be less concerned about your body movements around a room *(you'll most likely be sitting)*, but posture, facial expressions, and eye contact will be constantly monitored by your trainee. Likewise, you can monitor your trainee's nonverbal responses more effectively as well.

Keep in mind that you're a guide, taking your trainee through uncharted waters, coaching him to locate his destination. You may need to repeat the process a number of times, slowly allowing him to take control of the ship, until he can navigate on his own.

As in large group facilitation, quality support materials can help. Utilize discussions, always ask for questions and a restatement *(or demonstration)* of what was learned, and allow for plenty of practice.

As a one-on-one coach, you'll stand by until the individual you're training has acquired new knowledge, mastered a different skill, and/or adjusted his attitude. That's the beauty of one-on-one coaching. You're usually there to lend a hand after a day, or week, or month of training. You can monitor your results, encourage additional practice, and ensure success. If handled correctly, one-on-one coaching can be personally and professionally enriching.

In Honolulu...

After the initial training session, Andre planned to coach each line worker one-on-one. He chose Mick, the shy one, to be first. Andre sat down with Mick and questioned him about the training session, his job, and any further coaching he might need. The session was informative. Andre discovered that Mick was handling more than his share of the work, which contributed, in part, to his not carefully following the established toxic waste procedures. It appeared that Andre was coaching the wrong individual....

Establishing rapport will definitely ease the coaching process. That rapport will make it easier for you to field questions, get agreement on needs and goals, and help the trainee improve performance.

Group Facilitation

As with one-on-one coaching, establishing rapport with groups is important as well. Although rapport is usually established when you meet people for the first time, it can also be established successfully with members of a small group or team who have previously met you, but don't *"know you"* personally. Make sure you take the time to establish rapport in your own, unique way at the outset of any group session.

In Los Angeles...

In order to break the ice, Raylene and Max split up the group into smaller groups and rotated among them. Raylene joined a group of salespeople she was less familiar with. They were part-timers who primarily worked evenings, the shift Max covered. *"I'd like to get to know you better,"* Raylene began, and asked them for their names. *"Sales is not an easy job,"* she said. *"In fact, sometimes you run into embarrassing situations."* She continued by describing one of hers, then asked if any of the group members had a situation to share. Before long, they were all laughing....

As a coach who is facilitating learning in a larger group, your ability to facilitate good discussion can mean the difference between an effective and an ineffective session. Learn to facilitate good discussion among participants and watch your success rate climb. To become an effective facilitator, it is important to bear in mind the following:

1. Learn to wait before responding

Don't be *"quick on the draw"* after an individual makes a comment or observation, even if you're concerned about time constraints. It's critical that participants have an opportunity to verbalize what they intended to convey to the group. Besides, waiting a moment before responding allows others in the group to process what has just been said.

2. Redirect questions to the group

This may seem like a contradiction to what you learned earlier about fielding questions. But it's not. Sometimes being an effective facilitator means allowing others in the group to answer questions initially directed at you. As the facilitator, you always have the option to throw a question *"out to the group"* for feedback or discussion. This is an excellent technique to facilitate group involvement and benefit from the experiences of the participants.

3. Use the energy of the group

Sometimes a facilitating session can take on a life of its own. When this occurs, assess the situation. If you've gotten way off the beaten track, consider redirecting the group. Otherwise, utilize the energy of the group instead of resisting it. The key is your personal willingness to be influenced by the group, and your ability to facilitate beneficial discussion as a result. Avoid being so structured that you are unable to respond to what the group may need to focus on.

4. Provide positive reinforcement for participation

To continually encourage participation during discussion, be sure to recognize the contributions of participants when they share their opinions. Use affirmative statements like, *"Thank you for your ideas," "That's a good point,"* and *"I appreciate that comment."* Such statements are often welcome forms of feedback for the participant.

5. Avoid making judgmental statements

Making a judgmental statement, such as, *"That can't be right," "That's not very funny,"* or *"How can you believe that?"* to an individual will typically block the facilitation of further discussion. Be as diplomatic and sensitive as possible when responding to what participants have said. Effective facilitators are concerned about how they respond to those they're training.

In Los Angeles...

Max was leading a discussion of *"sizing up"* a customer, when the group got off topic and into the familiar controversy about whether salespeople should spend more time talking about surf or showing the customer different boards on the store racks. Max let the group continue. The discussion was insightful, and he knew he could return to his topic at any moment. He didn't want to stifle the group's enthusiasm, and after a few minutes, found an opportunity to summarize the key points and move on.

Whether you're applying your coaching and facilitating skills in one-on-one coaching or group facilitation, be aware that you're facilitating *"learning."* You're not there to put on a show or amaze an individual with your expertise, so utilize your skills accordingly. Work with individuals to apply their newfound knowledge and skills, establish rapport with team members so they'll listen to your ideas about increasing their job performance, and facilitate good discussion among participants in such a manner that they'll learn different ways to apply what you've just taught them. Successful coaching and facilitating is rewarding for both you and those whom you train.

Chapter Ten Worksheet: Increasing Your Effectiveness In Every Situation

1. You've just been promoted, and you must coach a newly hired individual to take over all of your current job responsibilities. Since this individual will be working for you, the more successful he or she is, the more helpful it'll be for you. Come up with a list of questions you want to ask this individual in your pre-coaching session.

2. You've been asked to train a team of individuals who aren't excited about the training venture. List two ways you can establish rapport with this team.

3. You're a very structured person, and the group you're training has a tendency to divert from your structure. How can you build in opportunities for growth and learning while keeping on schedule with your agenda?

Calculating Your Success

If you desire to improve the way you deliver training, you'll have to do more than read about it. You'll have to practice. Then you'll actually coach and facilitate, and then practice some more.

But how do you know what areas to practice? It's not enough to rely on your own sense of how well a session went. You may be able to accurately assess some points of your own delivery, but it's doubtful you can gauge every point from a participant's point of view.

You need feedback. Without feedback from those you coach, you'll flounder in a sea of uncertainty: *"Did I answer every question effectively? Was I flexible enough in facilitating discussions? Should I have paced the content differently? Were my overheads legible?"* The list goes on. Feedback on these and other components of program evaluation lets you know which skills to practice and improve upon.

Evaluating Core Competencies

Following is a list of *"core competencies"* for measuring facilitator effectiveness. Give your participants this worksheet *(see the Appendix for a form you can copy)*, and have them fill it out after the session. Each of the core competencies is scaled from 1 to 5, with 1 representing *"Not Effective"* and 5 representing *"Highly Effective."*

Core Competencies Evaluation

Rate each of the core competencies, which are scaled from 1 to 5. Number 1 represents *"Not Effective"* and 5 represents *"Highly Effective."*

Core Competencies	Demonstrated Effectiveness				
Training Methods	**Not Effective**			**Highly Effective**	
1. Effective introduction	1	2	3	4	5
2. Effective ice breaker	1	2	3	4	5
3. Establishes rapport	1	2	3	4	5
4. Examples emphasize key points	1	2	3	4	5
5. Knowledge of material	1	2	3	4	5
6. Demonstrates flexibility	1	2	3	4	5
7. Effective questioning	1	2	3	4	5
8. Answers questions effectively	1	2	3	4	5
9. Facilitates discussion	1	2	3	4	5
10. Manages participant behaviors	1	2	3	4	5
11. Makes smooth transitions	1	2	3	4	5
12. Effective explanations	1	2	3	4	5
13. Clear summaries	1	2	3	4	5
Facilitation Skills					
14. Encourages group participation	1	2	3	4	5
15. Checks for understanding	1	2	3	4	5
16. Effective use of training equipment	1	2	3	4	5
17. Exercise debrief	1	2	3	4	5
Verbal Skills					
18. Pleasant	1	2	3	4	5
19. Natural	1	2	3	4	5
20. Dynamic	1	2	3	4	5
21. Expressive	1	2	3	4	5
22. Easily heard	1	2	3	4	5
Nonverbal Skills					
23. Posture	1	2	3	4	5
24. Hand gestures	1	2	3	4	5
25. Body movements	1	2	3	4	5
26. Facial expressions	1	2	3	4	5
27. Eye contact	1	2	3	4	5
Trainer Support Materials					
28. Effective participant materials	1	2	3	4	5
29. Visible/effective flip chart	1	2	3	4	5
30. Visible/effective overheads	1	2	3	4	5
31. Visible/effective print material	1	2	3	4	5
32. Visible/effective video	1	2	3	4	5
33. Visible/effective slides	1	2	3	4	5

Adding up the ratings from the completed worksheets you receive will provide you with a good idea of what you need to work on. Start on the areas that need the most improvement. Keep a record of your scores and continue collecting feedback after every training session. If you persistently work on your skills, you should see an improvement in your evaluation scores.

Requesting Verbal Feedback

While written evaluations are valuable, supplementing them with verbal feedback can provide even better direction for improving your skills. A one-on-one coaching situation affords an ideal opportunity to ask for verbal feedback. You can also ask for feedback from small groups or teams, although you may be more comfortable *(and so might the participants)* if you ask for the feedback on an individual basis.

If you ask for verbal feedback, stay away from questions that are too general and questions that require only a yes or no answer. *"What did you think of the training session?"* isn't specific enough. Your evaluator might respond with, *"I thought it went well,"* or he might begin a lengthy exposition about how the training room needs to be modernized. Instead, compose questions that relate to the different skill areas *(e.g., How would you describe the pacing of my delivery? How effective were my explanations? How could the practice segments be improved?).*

Receiving Feedback Constructively

If you do ask for verbal feedback, it's helpful to consider the following tips for receiving feedback constructively:

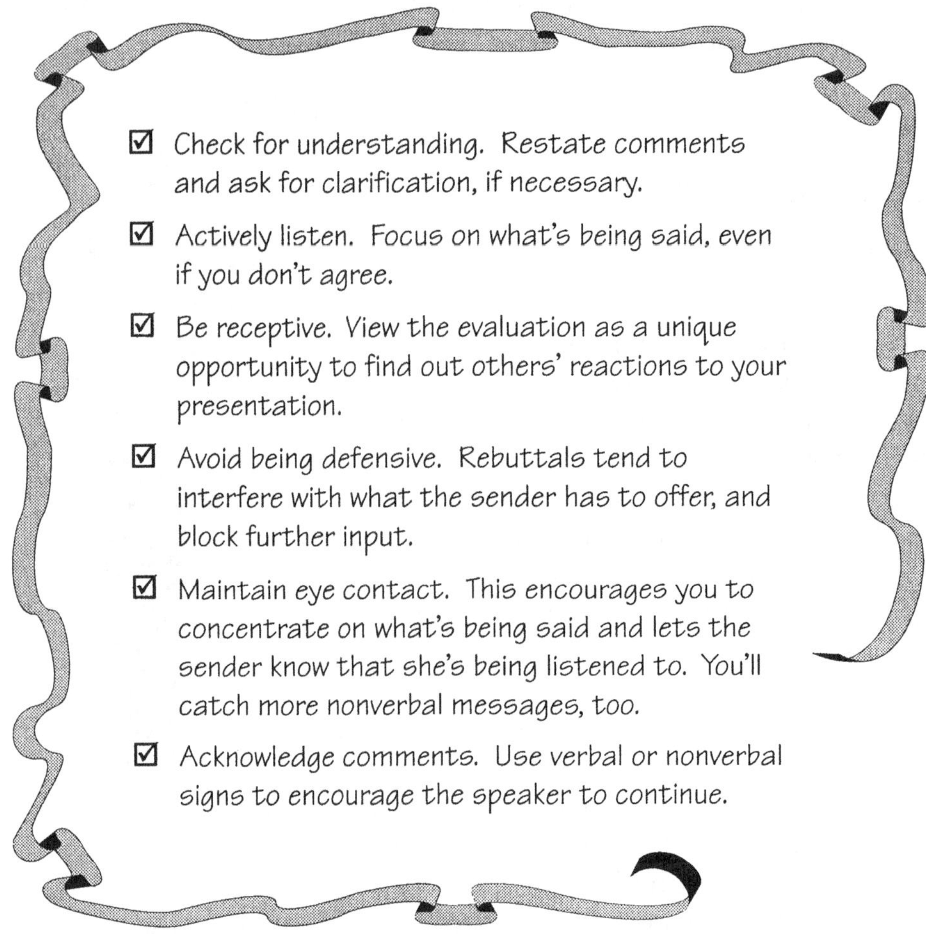

Feedback is an important component of the training process. Without it, your improvement efforts have a slimmer chance of actually strengthening your coaching and facilitating skills. With it, you're aimed in the right direction.

In Honolulu...

Andre passed out an evaluation form after his initial session with the four workers. The results proved helpful. All of the men found him very effective in explaining things clearly and effectively. In other areas, such as trainer support materials, Andre knew he'd have to work to improve his coaching/facilitating skills.

After the one-on-one coaching sessions, Andre also asked for oral feedback. Some of the men were more willing to share their feelings than others. For those more reticent, Andre asked specific questions. He discovered that his one-on-one coaching skills were definitely better than his skills in training small groups. Andre committed himself to practicing his facilitation skills. After all, this was his first actual *"training opportunity."* There were many more opportunities ahead.

In Los Angeles...

Raylene and Max had the salespeople complete an evaluation form for each of them. The results were quite good. Still, both Raylene and Max realized that their scores could be much higher. Raylene needed further practice on her delivery skills, and Max resolved to work more with support materials. They were eager to see how their salespeople handled the new custom ordering method.

Improvements to the bottom line

It's great to receive immediate feedback from trainees, but what really counts is how well the training improves their actual job performance.

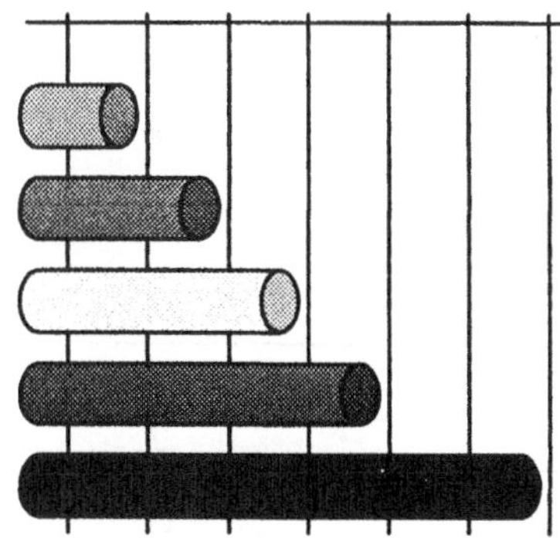

Checking back with your trainees and observing them in the weeks and months following training is critical to evaluating true training success. Focus on clear, measurable improvements in job performance and work outputs to identify gaps that require more attention. Check with customers to see if their satisfaction level has increased. For in-depth information on measuring the bottom-line, read *Measuring The Impact Of Training* in this series, *Training And Development.*

Chapter Eleven Worksheet: Improving Through Feedback

Considering feedback from peers or training participants, choose four core competencies you'd like to work on, and list specific ways you could improve the competencies *(e.g., for vocal variety, you might practice reading the newspaper aloud at home, offer to give a presentation at work, etc.).*

1. Competency # 1:
Ways to improve:

2. Competency # 2:
Ways to improve:

3. Competency # 3:
Ways to improve:

4. Competency # 4:
Ways to improve:

CHAPTER TWELVE

SUMMARY

It's not an easy route to successful coaching and facilitating. There are many detours, and sometimes it feels as if you're traveling the same road over and over. But that's the key to the journey. You need to know the road inside-out to make it to the same destination every time. As soon as you've mastered the signs along the way, you'll be assured of success.

First, you must complete your preparations. Then you'll employ successful verbal and nonverbal skills, develop and use your support materials effectively, and enhance your facilitation skills. Finally, remember to ask for feedback and use it to improve your performance. It's a method guaranteed to increase your success as a coach and facilitator.

Reproducible Forms And Worksheets

The pages in the Appendix are provided for you to photocopy and use appropriately.

Core Competencies Evaluation

Rate each of the core competencies, which are scaled from 1 to 5.
Number 1 represents *"Not Effective"* and 5 represents *"Highly Effective."*

Core Competencies	**Demonstrated Effectiveness**				
Training Methods	**Not Effective**			**Highly Effective**	
1. Effective introduction	1	2	3	4	5
2. Effective ice breaker	1	2	3	4	5
3. Establishes rapport	1	2	3	4	5
4. Examples emphasize key points	1	2	3	4	5
5. Knowledge of material	1	2	3	4	5
6. Demonstrates flexibility	1	2	3	4	5
7. Effective questioning	1	2	3	4	5
8. Answers questions effectively	1	2	3	4	5
9. Facilitates discussion	1	2	3	4	5
10. Manages participant behaviors	1	2	3	4	5
11. Makes smooth transitions	1	2	3	4	5
12. Effective explanations	1	2	3	4	5
13. Clear summaries	1	2	3	4	5
Facilitation Skills					
14. Encourages group participation	1	2	3	4	5
15. Checks for understanding	1	2	3	4	5
16. Effective use of training equipment	1	2	3	4	5
17. Exercise debrief	1	2	3	4	5
Verbal Skills					
18. Pleasant	1	2	3	4	5
19. Natural	1	2	3	4	5
20. Dynamic	1	2	3	4	5
21. Expressive	1	2	3	4	5
22. Easily heard	1	2	3	4	5
Nonverbal Skills					
23. Posture	1	2	3	4	5
24. Hand gestures	1	2	3	4	5
25. Body movements	1	2	3	4	5
26. Facial expressions	1	2	3	4	5
27. Eye contact	1	2	3	4	5
Trainer Support Materials					
28. Effective participant materials	1	2	3	4	5
29. Visible/effective flip chart	1	2	3	4	5
30. Visible/effective overheads	1	2	3	4	5
31. Visible/effective print material	1	2	3	4	5
32. Visible/effective video	1	2	3	4	5
33. Visible/effective slides	1	2	3	4	5

TRAINING EMPLOYEES ON FAMILIAR TASKS	
STEP	**EXPLANATION**
1. Describe The Area Of Needed Improvement	❑ Specifically explain how/why the employee's area of needed improvement affects on-the-job performance. Cite a specific and convincing example of a project or situation where you observed this limitation.
2. Solicit The Employee's Ideas And Perceptions	❑ Coach the employee to analyze his own behavior and take *"ownership"* of his actions and development plans. If the employee completely denies that a problem exists, tell him that you *"perceive"* there are areas that need improvement, and seek suggestions on how to change *your* perception.
3. React To The Employee's Ideas And Share Your Own Suggestions	❑ Reinforce the employee if he is *"on target,"* or redirect him if he is *"off the mark,"* by sharing alternative views that will lead toward your mutual objectives.
4. Seek A Common Development Plan And Summarize Key Steps For You And The Employee To Take	❑ The more involved the employee is in discussing and resolving the area of needed improvement, the more likely he is to be committed to a plan of action.
5. Schedule A Review Session	❑ Close on a positive note, communicating your confidence in the employee's success.

Training Employees On A New Task

Step	Explanation
1. Describe The Task	❑ How it fits into the existing department's system and processes ❑ Why it is important ❑ What you expect the employee to do upon completion of the training
2. Provide An Overview Of The Steps Required To Successfully Complete The Task	❑ Break down the task into sequential, logical steps to increase understanding and retention, while reducing anxiety ❑ Encourage the employee to take notes
3. Walk Through Each Step	❑ Explain the expected process and standards of performance ❑ When possible, show them how; otherwise, a verbal or mediated *(e.g. video, etc.)* "*tour*" will suffice ❑ Provide examples, suggestions, and "*what if*" scenarios ❑ Predict potential problems and assist the employee with how to deal with the unexpected ❑ Describe which steps are flexible and which are not
4. Observe Your Employee Completing The Sequence Of Steps	❑ Check for understanding and comfort ❑ Recognize that it's normal to be anxious or make mistakes ❑ Avoid embarrassing the employee
5. Provide Feedback	❑ Reinforce positive behaviors; catch them doing something right! ❑ Remain patient; don't expect perfection; avoid being overly critical; allow for mistakes ❑ Encourage the employee to ask questions throughout the process
6. Schedule A Review Session	❑ Allow adequate time for mastery or surfacing of ideas/concerns ❑ Keep an "*open-door*" policy for questions, concerns, and suggestions

ON-THE-JOB TRAINING PLAN

Employee:	Training Objectives:
Performance Outcomes:	Training Methods:

WHAT
- specific actions/topics

WHO
- trainer
- trainee(s)
- evaluator(s)

HOW
- required time
- budget
- materials
- equipment

WHEN/WHERE
- schedule
- location

WHY
- reasons
- benefits
- expectations
- measurements

Professional And Personal Development Publications From Richard Chang Associates, Inc.

Designed to support continuous learning, these highly targeted, integrated collections from Richard Chang Associates, Inc. (RCA) help individuals and organizations acquire the knowledge and skills needed to succeed in today's ever-changing workplace. Titles are available through RCA, Jossey-Bass, Inc., fine bookstores, and distributors internationally.

Practical Guidebook Collection

Quality Improvement Series

Continuous Process Improvement
Continuous Improvement Tools, Volume 1
Continuous Improvement Tools, Volume 2
Step-By-Step Problem Solving
Meetings That Work!
Improving Through Benchmarking
Succeeding As A Self-Managed Team
Measuring Organizational Improvement Impact
Process Reengineering In Action
Satisfying Internal Customers First!

Management Skills Series

Interviewing And Selecting High Performers
On-The-Job Orientation And Training
Coaching Through Effective Feedback
Expanding Leadership Impact
Mastering Change Management
Re-Creating Teams During Transitions
Planning Successful Employee Performance
Coaching For Peak Employee Performance
Evaluating Employee Performance

High Performance Team Series

Success Through Teamwork
Building A Dynamic Team
Measuring Team Performance
Team Decision-Making Techniques

High-Impact Training Series

Creating High-Impact Training
Identifying Targeted Training Needs
Mapping A Winning Training Approach
Producing High-Impact Learning Tools
Applying Successful Training Techniques
Measuring The Impact Of Training
Make Your Training Results Last

Workplace Diversity Series

Capitalizing On Workplace Diversity
Successful Staffing In A Diverse Workplace
Team Building For Diverse Work Groups
Communicating In A Diverse Workplace
Tools For Valuing Diversity

Personal Growth And Development Collection

Managing Your Career in a Changing Workplace
Unlocking Your Career Potential
Marketing Yourself and Your Career
Making Career Transitions
Memory Tips For The Forgetful

101 Stupid Things Collection

101 Stupid Things Trainers Do To Sabotage Success
101 Stupid Things Supervisors Do To Sabotage Success
101 Stupid Things Employees Do To Sabotage Success
101 Stupid Things Salespeople Do To Sabotage Success
101 Stupid Things Business Travelers Do To Sabotage Success

About Richard Chang Associates, Inc.

Richard Chang Associates, Inc. (RCA) is a multi-disciplinary organizational performance improvement firm. Since 1987, RCA has provided private and public sector clients around the world with the experience, expertise, and resources needed to build capability in such critical areas as process improvement, management development, project management, team performance, performance measurement, and facilitator training. RCA's comprehensive package of services, products, and publications reflect the firm's commitment to practical, innovative approaches and to the achievement of significant, measurable results.

RCA Resources Optimize Organizational Performance

Consulting — Using a broad range of skills, knowledge, and tools, RCA consultants assist clients in developing and implementing a wide range of performance improvement initiatives.

Training — Practical, "real world" training programs are designed with a "take initiative" emphasis. Options include off-the-shelf programs, customized programs, and public and on-site seminars.

Curriculum And Materials Development — A cost-effective and flexible alternative to internal staffing, RCA can custom-develop and/or customize content to meet both organizational objectives and specific program needs.

Video Production — RCA's award-winning, custom video productions provide employees with information in a consistent manner that achieves lasting impact.

Publications — The comprehensive and practical collection of publications from RCA supports organizational training initiatives and self-directed learning.

Packaged Programs — Designed for first-time and experienced trainers alike, these programs offer comprehensive, integrated materials (including selected Practical Guidebooks) that provide a wide range of flexible training options. Choose from:

- Meetings That Work! ToolPAK™
- Step-By-Step Problem Solving ToolKIT™
- Continuous Process Improvement Packaged Training Program
- Continuous Improvement Tools, Volume 1 ToolPAK™
- Continuous Improvement Tools, Volume 2 ToolPAK™
- High Involvement Teamwork™ Packaged Training Program

RICHARD
CHANG
ASSOCIATES

World Class Resources. World Class Results.℠

Richard Chang Associates, Inc.
Corporate Headquarters
15265 Alton Parkway, Suite 300, Irvine, California 92618 USA
(800) 756-8096 • (949) 727-7477 • Fax: (949) 727-7007
E-Mail: info@rca4results.com • www.richardchangassociates.com

U.S. Offices in Irvine and Atlanta • Licensees and Distributors Worldwide

Printed and bound by CPI Group (UK) Ltd, Croydon, CR0 4YY
09/06/2025
14685915-0005